Media Econom

Key Concerns in Media Studies

Series Editor: Andrew Crisell

Within the context of today's global, digital environment, *Key Concerns in Media Studies* addresses themes and concepts that are integral to the study of media. Concisely written by leading academics, the books consider the historical development of these themes and the theories that underpin them, and assess their overall significance, using up-to-date examples and case studies throughout. By giving a clear overview of each topic, the series provides an ideal starting point for all students of modern media.

Published

Forthcoming

Media Economics

Stuart Cunningham
Terry Flew
and
Adam Swift

First published 2015 by
PALGRAVE

Palgrave in the UK is an imprint of Macmillan Publishers Limited, registered in England, company number 785998, of 4 Crinan Street, London N1 9XW.

Palgrave Macmillan in the US is a division of St Martin's Press LLC, 175 Fifth Avenue, New York, NY 10010.

Palgrave is a global imprint of the above companies and is represented throughout the world.

Palgrave® and Macmillan® are registered trademarks in the United States, the United Kingdom, Europe and other countries.

ISBN 978–0–230–29322–9

This book is printed on paper suitable for recycling and made from fully managed and sustained forest sources. Logging, pulping and manufacturing processes are expected to conform to the environmental regulations of the country of origin.

A catalogue record for this book is available from the British Library.

A catalog record for this book is available from the Library of Congress.

Printed and bound by CPI Group (UK) Ltd, Croydon, CR0 4YY

Library of Congress Cataloging-in-Publication Data

Cunningham, Stuart.
  Media economics / Stuart Cunningham, Terry Flew, Adam Swift.
    pages cm
  Includes bibliographical references.
  ISBN 978-0-230-29322-9
  1. Mass media--Economic aspects. 2. Mass media--Economic aspects--Case studies. I. Flew, Terry. II. Swift, Adam. III. Title.
  P96.E25C86 2015
  338.4'730223--dc23
                                        2015003832

Contents

Tables and Figures

Tables

Figures

Acknowledgements

Research on which this book is based was in part supported by the Australian Research Council through its funding of the ARC Centre of Excellence for Creative Industries and Innovation (SR0590002) and through the ARC Discovery Project (110101455), Informal Economics and Audiovisual Industries: Histories, Dynamics, Legal and Policy Responses, awarded to Julian Thomas, Stuart Cunningham, Ramon Lobato and Dan Hunter.

We would like to thank the *Key Concerns in Media Studies* series editor, Andrew Crisell, and Palgrave Commissioning Editor Lloyd Langman for their support and expert advice, and the anonymous referees who engaged very helpfully with the book in manuscript form. Thanks also to Bonnie Liu Rui for her work in assisting research for the book.

The authors and publishers thank the copyright holders for permission to reproduce the following:

> Table I.2 from Ballon, P. (2014) 'Old and New Issues in Media Economics', in K. Donders, C. Pauwels and J. Loisen (eds.), *The Palgrave Handbook of European Media Policy* (p.76). Basingstoke: Palgrave. Reproduced with permission of Palgrave.
>
> Table 3.1 from Williamson, O. E. (2000) 'The New Institutional Economics: Taking Stock, Looking Ahead'. *Journal of Economic Literature* 38: 595–613. Reproduced with permission of Oliver E. Williamson and the American Economic Association.
>
> Figure 3.1 adapted from Loisen, J. (2012) 'Prospects and Pitfalls for Douglas North's New Institutional Economics Approach for Global Media Policy Research', in N. Just and M. Puppis (eds.), *Trends in Communication Policy Research: New Theories, methods and Subjects* (pp. 35–3). Bristol: Intellect. Reproduced with permission of Intellect Books.

Introduction

This is a book on media economics aimed at scholars, teachers and students in media, cultural and communication studies, as well as anyone interested in how to make sense of rapid change in the media environment. A background in economics is not necessary, but an interest in issues that have an economic dimension is. Many discussions in media and related fields draw upon economic concepts, assumptions and histories while dealing with industry sectors that are, in many ways, at the forefront of structural economic change in post-industrial/advanced capitalist societies.

There is a general agreement that understanding the economic dynamics of media industries and markets is vitally important for the analysis of the media system as a whole. In this book, we do not attempt a comprehensive coverage of all topics covered by media economics. In such a short book, that is completely impractical, and there are already numerous primers which cover mainstream issues in the field very well (for example, Picard, 1989; Albarran 2002, 2010; Alexander *et al.*, 2004; De Vany, 2004; Hoskins *et al.*, 2004; Doyle, 2006, 2013; Mosco, 2009; Hardy, 2014). Here, we have attempted to outline the key elements of the mainstream literature and to complement that literature by pointing to what we believe to be traditions in economics that have been neglected in the field as it is applied to the media.

At regular intervals, we develop case studies to indicate that these different economic paradigms are not just theories but also provide important practical insights that illustrate the utility of considering diverse approaches in economics. These case studies (which appear inside boxed text in the first four chapters) and extended case studies (Chapter 5) address enduring, central topics and substantive issues with which media, communication and cultural studies curricula and students routinely engage. These include basics about supply and demand in media markets; concentration of media ownership; the challenges for media economics of digital platforms; the different ways economic, political and cultural power is exercised through media; contracts and broadcasting property rights; governing media in an age of globalisation; media piracy; and an extended consideration of the future of public service media and the rapid emergence of a post-broadcast television ecology.

Having said that, we offer a distinctive way of organising an introduction to media economics. We do this because what *counts* as an important issue in media economics is strongly influenced by the framework or theoretical tradition being employed. We identify, in Chapters 1 and 2, the two main strands that dominate our understanding of media economics and which contend for overall legitimacy in the field: neoclassical, or mainstream, media economics and critical political economy of the media. These two variants deserve to be treated as the reigning orthodoxies as they produce powerful analyses of the way media works. But they are in many ways so divergent in terms of their objects of analysis, their methodologies and their founding assumptions that a conscientious student, coming at the topic from the disciplines of media, cultural and communication studies, may find that such a divergence makes it difficult to get to grips with media economics. Moreover, neither approach has typically held a particularly charitable view towards the other. Mainstream media economics, like economics more generally, has rarely acknowledged much that is of value in critical approaches to the field, while critical political economy has not only defined itself in opposition to the mainstream approaches, but has at times presented those approaches, and the media economists who use them, as being politically regressive and lacking in an ethic of the common good.

Economics as a field emerged in the context of the European Enlightenment and the Industrial Revolution, with Adam Smith's *The Wealth of Nations* (1991 [1776]) being a key formative text. The divide between what we now know as neoclassical economics, on the one hand, and critical political economy, on the other, can be traced as far back to the different paths followed in the field from the 1850s onwards between the 'marginal revolution', on the one hand, and the work of Karl Marx and the socialist economists, on the other. A broad overview of the differences between the mainstream and critical approaches, which we will elaborate upon in this book, is shown in Table I.1.[1]

Economics as a field is more complex than this dualism captures. The rise of Keynesian macroeconomics (Keynes, 1936) in the wake of the 1930s Great Depression introduced a method that 'wished to save the essentials of the capitalist system but realised that this could only be done within the framework of a strong and systematically interventionist state' (Hobsbawm, 1979, p. 245). There have remained a series of approaches associated with reformist perspectives in political

Table I.1   Differences between mainstream economics and critical political economy

Mainstream economics	Critical political economy
Focus on the individual	Focus on collective entities (e.g. social classes)
Individual rational choice	Socially determined belief systems
Analysis of market exchange	Analysis of circuits of production, distribution and consumption
Study of market equilibrium situations (micro)	Study of socio-historical processes (macro)
Focus on individual choices and mutual benefits of interaction through markets	Focus on power, social conflict and forms of collective agency
Economics as a stand-alone discipline	Political economy as inherently interdisciplinary
Preference for formal models and quantitative methods	Preference for descriptive analysis and qualitative methods
Scholarship as a value-neutral activity (separation of facts and values)	Scholarship as a form of political and ethical engagement (facts and values interconnected)
Markets lead to social harmony	Capitalism based on social conflict

Source: Derived from Stilwell (2002, pp. 155) and Earl and Peng (2012, pp. 458–60).

economy, including institutionalist and post-Keynesian economics, as well as challenges to the hegemony of neoclassical theory from the perspectives of behavioural economics, innovation economics and new institutionalism, which we will consider in this book (Cole *et al.*, 1991; Stilwell, 2002).[2]

Media economics also presents its specific challenges, as the media have many distinctive attributes that challenge traditional microeconomic modelling and theories of supply and demand. These include the social and political objectives attached to media to promote quality, diversity and pluralism, the nature of information goods in the public domain, the cultural contribution of media content and the power associated with concentrated media ownership and media conglomerates, including the capacity to influence politics and public opinion. Ballon (2014) has provided an overview of distinctive features of media economics (Table I.2).

Understanding media through the prism of media economics requires that we broaden the scope of approaches that are considered,

Table I.2 Neoclassical economics assumptions and media economics

Neoclassical economics assumptions	Media economic characteristics
Main objective: efficient production, distribution and consumption of scarce goods	Main objective: besides efficiency, also quality, diversity, pluralism and innovation. Information and opinions not really scarce
Tends to focus on private goods	Information goods have a (semi) public character
Products are homogeneous, i.e., interchangeable	Products are unique
Marginal cost is significant	Marginal cost very low/close to zero
Focus on price competition	Price competition secondary or non-existent
Owners are rational profit maximisers	Owners seek societal and political influence
Policy intervenes based on market failure	Policy intervenes also without invoking market failure, including contribution to public debate, citizenship, societal health/wealth

Source: Ballon (2014, p. 76). Reproduced with permission of Palgrave.

as new developments in media industries and markets are stretching the capacity of the established neoclassical and critical political economy paradigms. The new dynamics of media production and consumption involve developments such as the generalisation of convergent digital media platforms across all media; the growing interest in the socio-economic value of networks; the disruptive implications of digital media technologies on long established media business models; the rise of user-generated media content through YouTube and other social media and the need to reconceptualise the nature of media audiences; and the growth of creative industries policy discourse, with its focus on media and cultural sectors as sources of wealth creation and economic innovation.

It is our contention – and the main reason for adding this book to the already substantial literature on media economics – that there are schools in the rich and deep history and contemporary practice of economics that have rarely, if ever, been applied to the media which may help us in dealing with the 'new realities' in the economics of the media today. In this book we will focus upon institutional economics and evolutionary economics – strands of what in the discipline gets called 'heterodox' economics, which are alternatives to mainstream neoclassicism and critical political economy (Earl and Peng, 2012).

Of course, we are not the only ones making this point. The media economist Steven Wildman, who was chief economist with the United States Federal Communications Commission (FCC) from 2012 to 2014, has made the point that while neoclassical economics is at the cornerstone of mainstream media economics, and is still 'the source of the intuition guiding much, if not most, of today's economic research', it is also the case that 'the neoclassical approach... [is] no longer the overwhelmingly dominant paradigm it once was' (Wildman, 2006, p. 68). Reviewing the field, Pieter Ballon (2014) has argued that several varieties of heterodox economics are required to supplement the insights that may be provided by the neoclassical paradigm, especially with the advent of new media technologies:

> While the typical static efficiency analysis and its extensions of neoclassical economics can have their application in the media, the field also has much to gain from so-called heterodox economics. Most prominently, an economic approach to the media needs to be informed by information economics, and network economics, institutional economics and evolutionary or innovation economics.
>
> (2014, p. 76)

Institutional and evolutionary economics are treated in Chapters 3 and 4 (and the others Ballon mentions also), but since they are rarely mentioned in media, communication and cultural studies, they need a short introduction here.

Institutional economics – as practised, for example, by Nobel Prize winners such as Douglass North, Oliver Williamson and Elinor Ostrom – emphasises the embedded nature of markets and the importance of institutions to economic growth and development. It is argued that the transactional dynamics which occur in markets cannot be captured with quantitative methods and comparative static equilibrium models alone; they are entangled with the social, cultural, political and technical conditions that make them possible. Understanding the institutional conditions for the formation and maintenance of markets, as well as the governance of firms, connects economics to complementary disciplines in the social sciences and the humanities (history, for example) and reminds us that markets are not totalising blocks of supervening power but are contingent, variable and often fragile. But they are also where most wealth is generated and it is through the mechanisms of which – for better or for worse – we dare say most students who pass through media, communication and cultural studies classrooms will earn a living.

Evolutionary economics offers a substantial alternative to critical political economy and is based on a model of the effects, bad and good, of living under capitalism that is as dynamically conflictual as its Marxist counterpart – with which, in its devotion to analysing the roots of economic and industrial change, it shares surprising continuities (Catephores, 1994; Rosenberg, 2011). This model is carried in the term 'creative destruction', which has become virtually synonymous with the work of Austrian-American economist Joseph Schumpeter since his major prognostications on the future of *Capitalism, Socialism and Democracy* (1942). The concept of creative destruction captures the degree to which capitalism is 'by nature a form or method of economic change and not only never is but never can be stationary' (Schumpeter, 1942, p. 82). The dynamic interaction between competition, innovation and business entrepreneurship 'incessantly revolutionises the economic structure from within, incessantly destroying the old one, incessantly creating a new one. This process of Creative Destruction is the essential fact about capitalism' (Schumpeter, 1942, p. 83). The idea is powerful because it insists that 'accumulation' (progress, wealth creation, technological innovation, etc.) and 'annihilation' (business failure, cycles of boom and bust, environmental degradation, etc.) are mutually constitutive forces.

Heterodox forms of economics do not typically feature at the core of the economics discipline, but they do constitute a fundamental reframing of the neoclassical orthodoxy. They have also provided the foundations for policy-oriented research in areas with clear implications for the media, such as innovation policy, governance structures for public institutions, policies towards media ownership and approaches to support research into new media content and services. For those in media, communication and cultural studies interested in better understanding the dynamics of socio-technical change in what Manuel Castells (1996) has termed 'informational capitalism', it is important to recognise that there is far more 'ferment in the field' in economics than would be assumed from relying upon reference points in the well-staged opposition between neoclassical economics and critical political economy.

Another reason why we argue in this book that media, communication and cultural studies need to revisit media economics in its various forms is that such disciplines have often held a static and one-dimensional account of what economics is. It is wrongly assumed that the field of economics is relatively homogeneous in its scope and methods; economics as represented in undergraduate courses and standard textbook constitutes the leading edges of thought in the discipline; and economic methodologies easily map onto particular political orthodoxies. The latter premise is sometimes stated in terms of neoclassical economics being synonymous with a form of neoliberal politics that is inimical to both understanding the intrinsic value of culture and engaging with what matters in the critical humanities.

Leading figures in media, communication and cultural studies from both political economy and cultural studies have come to question the one-dimensional account of economics that has become something of a critical orthodoxy. The leading cultural studies theorist Lawrence Grossberg observed in *Cultural Studies in the Future Tense* that

> [t]he apparent inability or unwillingness to criticize economics as useful knowledge from anything but a radically external position produces an extreme disconnection between socio-cultural criticism and the world of economics. Too often, the criticism of academic economics is founded on an imaginary summation, which is really a relative ignorance, of economics; in addition, the point from which such criticisms are offered is often not a theorised analysis of real economic complexities, but an imagined position of radical opposition, in which the only possible politics is defined by the moral project of overthrowing capitalism.
>
> (Grossberg, 2010, p. 107)

Nicholas Garnham, one of the founders of the critical political economy of media approach, has also called for a re-evaluation of the contributions of mainstream economics to media, communication and cultural studies. Garnham has expressed concern that the critical tradition has ossified in its understanding of the dynamics of capitalist economies in recent years, arguing that what he refers to as 'a romantic Marxist rejection of the market *per se*' has 'blocked analysis of how actual markets work and with what effects. This has meant that ... it has not taken the economics in PE [political economy] with the seriousness that it deserves and requires' (Garnham, 2011, p. 42).

And it is happening as significant ferment in economics is also occurring. About 20% of Nobel Prizes in Economics over the past 20 years have been awarded to scholars outside the neoclassical paradigm. These include, for example, Elinor Ostrom, who did such brilliant work disproving the 'tragedy of the commons', showing how human collective action can defeat individualism and statism in the management of natural resources (Ostrom, 1990), and Amartya Sen, whose 'capabilities' approach to human well-being has revolutionised the concerns of development economics. They also include Nobel Prizes awarded to scholars in institutional economics such as Douglass North and Oliver Williamson, and economists who have combined a refinement of neo-Keynesian analytical techniques with interventions into global economic debates as progressive public intellectuals, such as Joseph Stiglitz and Paul Krugman. In short, we need to get a handle on schools in economics which have informed contemporary critiques of the dominant neoclassical paradigm, and the scope of such work goes considerably wider than the neo-Marxist political economy which, as Lawrence Grossberg (2010, p. 106) observes, has constituted the 'more agreeable writings about the economy' for critical scholars in media, communication and cultural studies.

What the book covers

This short book begins with an overview of the main strands of media economics. Chapter 1 deals with mainstream media economics, as it has been shaped by neoclassical theories. It identifies elements of the media that generate divergences from textbook microeconomics, including the diverse nature of media products, advertiser financing of commercial media, tendencies towards ownership concentration, the social shaping of consumer behaviour, the complexities of creative production and the role played by governments in regulating media as public goods. We argue that while such features of media make economic modelling along neoclassical lines more complex than it may be for other industries, this does not negate the validity of the approach in more general terms, and this is illustrated with a discussion of competition in changing digital media markets. But the question of realism is not the only line of critique of neoclassical approaches. More substantive issues arise in considering the methodological foundations of the neoclassical approach and its core propositions of methodological individualism, rational choice theory and equilibrium modelling, and how these in turn relate to a relatively 'closed' approach to applying analytical insights derived from other disciplines. These points are discussed in detail, but it is also noted that there may be differences here between mainstream economics as it appears in textbooks, or in relatively peripheral fields in the discipline such as media economics, and the debates that are taking place at the leading edges of the discipline, where many of the critiques of the neoclassical model are acknowledged.

Chapter 2 discusses the critical political economy approach to media, which is perhaps the best known among those in media, communication and cultural studies. We draw attention to the extent to which this is a diverse and dynamic field, albeit one with some core propositions around: the importance of understanding historical processes of social change; a sense of the mutually constitutive relationship between economic, social and cultural institutions, relations and practices; a moral philosophy oriented towards critiquing the industrial structures and social relations of capitalism; and a commitment to linking intellectual work with progressive social movements. We identify a tension in the field between a desire for inclusiveness of diverse research paradigms within the political economy 'tent' – Winseck (2011) identifies institutional, evolutionary and elements of neoclassical economics as being broadly cognate with political economy – and a contrary view among leading practitioners that political economy is defined in opposition to other research traditions. One site through which such debates were (at times acrimoniously) played out was around audience studies, between the 'active audience' strands of cultural studies and the critiques of such accounts as 'cultural populism'. More recently, some critical political economists have sought to distance the paradigm from various new directions in media industries research, including creative industries approaches and media production studies. We argue that a key to understanding critical political economy is through questions concerning power, and particularly the relationship between economic, political and cultural power.

Chapters 3 and 4 outline the core features of institutional and evolutionary economics respectively. As we assume that these will be the approaches least familiar to most of our readers, we take time to provide detailed expositions of core points before extending into application of these ideas into ways of understanding contemporary media. In the case of institutional economics in Chapter 3, we note that there is both 'old' and 'new' institutional economics, as well as institutional approaches in the social sciences generally, and sociology in particular, with which there are both family resemblances and ongoing differences: the continuing influence of Max Weber's work is relevant in this regard. We apply institutional economics to an understanding of contracts in the creative industries, the nature of broadcast media property and global media policy.

In the case of evolutionary economics, as discussed in Chapter 4, we note its influence in related fields such as information and innovation economics. We consider its significance in generating models of the relation of media and creative industries to the economy as a whole, an understanding of media and cultural markets as complex signalling devices and the relationship between market and non-market (household) production, whose co-evolutionary dynamics have given rise, for example, to the phenomenon of 'social network markets'. Further structural change in the economy has been reshaping our thinking about the relationship between commodities and 'gifts', and the issue of media piracy in the context of complex relations between intellectual property and innovation, where there is little consensus among economists about legal and policy implications.

Chapter 5 concludes the book with two detailed case studies that aim to bring together insights from the different fields of economics discussed in this book. The first is that of public service media (PSM). We argue that while the neoclassical approach, based on market failure, continues to have policy relevance, it does suffer from the absence of an institutional and historical perspective. The critical political economy approach, we propose, has come to be overly normative in its analysis of PSM, losing sight of the similarities in practice – as distinct from in theory – between PSMs and their commercial counterparts, as well as excessive claims about the uniqueness of PSMs. To take one example, the claim that PSMs are the sole providers of quality and diverse media content is increasingly untenable in a multichannel and convergent media environment. It is proposed that the new institutional economics (NIE) provide important insights into PSM in practice that warrant further consideration, but that an understanding of the pros and cons of new performance metrics being applied to PSM by policy-makers, such as public value tests, also need to be informed by insights from innovation economics.

The second case study is that of the changing ecology of television, whose distinctive features are most apparent in the US context. We argue that there is indeed Schumpeterian 'gales of creative destruction' descending upon the traditional media industries, driven by the emergent digital players such as Google, Apple, Amazon and Netflix. They are not only providing different platforms from which to view television – which is in turn setting off policy debates worldwide about whether governments are obliged to protect incumbent broadcasters – but also transforming the business models of television itself, using data analytics to drive production decisions as well as content distribution strategies. We note that the different perspectives considered in this book provide particular insights into this 'revolutionisation of television', but argue that it is in the integration of such diverse insights, rather than the maintenance of disciplinary intellectual silos, that the dynamics of such changes can be best understood and their wider implications more adequately theorised.

1 Media Economics: The Mainstream Approach

The field of media economics has existed in some form since the 1950s, and overviews can be found in Picard (1989), Alexander *et al.* (2004), Hoskins *et al.* (2004), Albarran (2002, 2010), Doyle (2006, 2013) and the *Journal of Media Economics*, which commenced publication in 1988. Media economics has been defined as being 'concerned with how media operators meet the informational and entertainment wants and needs of audiences, advertisers and society with available resources' (Picard, 1989, p. 7), and with 'the study of how media industries use scarce resources to produce content that is distributed among consumers in a society to satisfy various wants and needs' (Albarran, 2002, p. 5).

While economics has not been as central to the study of the media as communication studies, sociology and cultural studies, it has always had great significance beyond academia. One key reason is that it aims to capture how the media works from the perspective of those who run media businesses and make media policies. Gillian Doyle makes the point that 'economics, as a discipline, is highly relevant to understanding how media firms and industries operate... [because] most of the decisions taken by those who run media organisations are, to a greater or lesser extent, influenced by resource and financial issues' (Doyle, 2013, p. 1).

Media economics has been based around the mainstream definition of economics as 'the study of how people and society end up choosing... to employ scarce productive resources that could have alternative uses, to produce various commodities and distribute them... among various persons and groups in society' (Samuelson, 1976, p. 3). Following the pioneering analysis of Adam Smith in *The Wealth of Nations* (Smith 1991 [1776]) of what he termed the 'invisible hand', and the benefits to society to be derived from self-interested individual behaviour, economists have tended to prefer market allocation of resources to allocation based upon state planning or custom and tradition, as market relations 'permit mutually advantageous exchanges and ensure the efficient allocation of resources' (Stilwell, 2002, p. 147). In his account of Smith's work in *The Worldly Philosophers*, Robert Heilbroner summarised the case for the market system in these terms:

> Each should do what was to his best monetary advantage. In the market system the lure of gain, not the pull of tradition or the whip of authority, steered the great majority to his (or her) task. And yet, although each was free to go wherever his acquisitive nose directed him, the interplay of one person against another resulted in the necessary tasks of society getting done.
>
> (Heilbroner, 1999, pp. 20–21)

Media economics has drawn upon the neoclassical approach to the study of economics, or what is termed 'microeconomics', which involves the study of individual markets, as distinct from macroeconomics that deals with the study of national economies in the context of global trade. Various assumptions underpin the neoclassical approach to the study of media economics, including a focus on the individual as the primary object of analysis; the assumption that individuals engage in rational behaviour in order to maximise their benefits from market transactions; the expectation that markets will reach an optimal price, or an equilibrium point; and the assumption that this equilibrium point will be one that maximises benefits to both producers and consumers as a consequence of engaging in free exchange.

Such assumptions lead to the *theory of supply and demand*, a cornerstone of conventional microeconomics. This theory assumes that individual consumers are rational in their *demand* for goods and services which means that, all other things being equal, the lower the price, the more that is demanded. Similarly, the firms who *supply* such goods and services seek to maximise their profits (revenues minus costs), which means that the higher the price, the more they will supply. This produces what is known as the *equilibrium* point, where an upward-sloping supply curve and a downward-sloping demand curve meet at a particular price point where the quantity demanded meets the quantity supplied. If the price goes up, demand will fall, and if it goes down, demand will increase. These core concepts of economic theory are discussed in detail in any undergraduate economics textbook (e.g. Stilwell, 2002, pp. 151–54), as well as in the media economics texts noted above.

Markets in action: The case of tablet PCs

The launch of the Apple iPad in March 2010 was one of the most successful new product launches in the history of this highly innovative company. While Apple founder Steve Jobs was not a fan of market research, believing that consumers could not know whether or not they would want a product they had not seen, the company correctly surmised that there was significant consumer demand for a portable computing device that had a screen size similar to that of a personal computer, but the mobility and functionality of a mobile phone. Apple sold over 15 million iPads in the first 12 months of the product's existence, and while others produced similar products, they could not match the design and functionality of Apple's product: by the end of 2010, Apple accounted for 75% of the market share for tablet PCs.

In terms of market theory, Apple had created a situation in the new tablet PC market where demand exceeded supply, and consumers were prepared to pay a premium price for the Apple iPad over other tablet PCs. As a result, prices were relatively high for the first generation Apple iPads ($US499–829), and they were a highly profitable product for Apple. There were periods in 2011 where Apple was the world's largest company as measured by share market value, and at one point its cash reserves were greater than those of the US government.

Neoclassical economic theory predicts that in a situation where one company is earning above-average profits in a market, but there are no barriers to entry for new competitors, there will be entry of new competitors into that market, which will place downward pressure on prices. During 2011, this is indeed what happened, with the launch of the Samsung Galaxy Tab as well as tablet PCs by Acer, Asus, Lenovo, Sony, Toshiba and others. These were invariably cheaper than the Apple iPad: the cost of an entry-level Samsung Galaxy Tab in 2011 was $US299, as compared to $US499 for the Apple iPad 2. But equally importantly, they ran on a common operating system – the Google Android system – that enabled third parties such as apps developers to be able to produce apps that could be used on a wide range of branded tablet PCs, and achieve the economies of scale that existed in producing apps for Apple's iOS operating system.

By 2012, Apple's share of the tablet PC market had fallen to 40%, and by 2013 it was 30%. Apple responded to the challenge of

(Continued)

Samsung and others by launching the iPad Mini in 2012, which was a smaller version of the iPad that was priced at a level closer to that of its competitors. The market for tablet PCs continued to grow, with Google and Amazon developing their own products, and Microsoft developing a tablet/PC hybrid with the Surface Pro. In 2013, there were at least 195 million tablet PCs sold, as compared to 60 million in 2011, and the market for tablet PCs continues to grow. The key points illustrated by the market for tablet PCs are:

- With the introduction of the iPad in 2010, Apple created a new market for tablet PCs, where demand consistently exceeded supply, and the iPad was the preferred product. As a result, Apple was able to earn above-average profits.
- This, in turn, promoted its competitors to develop their own tablet PCs, which successfully competed with Apple on both price and product attributes.
- The average price of tablet PCs has fallen as competition has increased, while the range and diversity of types of tablet PC products available has increased.
- Apple has been forced to innovate in response to loss of market share, particularly by developing lower cost versions of its own tablet PC product.

An example of how media economics can approach a media-related question can be seen with debates about whether the media is 'dumbing down' the public through an excessive number of light entertainment programmes on TV, which are not seen as contributing to a more culturally and intellectually aware population. A version of this debate has existed for over a century (Bennett, 1982), and economists would not typically try to judge whether or not particular media content is of a high or low 'quality', leaving such questions to other disciplines. Economists would, however, relate the choices that media companies make about content to consumer preferences and would typically note that the media content referred to exists because audiences have demonstrated a preference for it: if those preferences change, so too will the content. While the resulting mix of media content may be optimal from the point of view of individual media producers and consumers, it may not be the most socially desirable according to other criteria, such as civic values or the promotion of an engaged citizenry and a vibrant public sphere. This would be seen as an instance of what economists term *market failure*, which refers to 'the failure of the market to advance socially desirable goals other than efficiency, e.g. preserving democracy and social cohesion' (Doyle, 2013, p. 92). If governments and policy-makers perceive a problem in a market-driven media environment, there are ways in which they can use public funding to ensure that other forms of media content is made available. Government funding of non-commercial *public service broadcasting* has historically been looked to as a means of addressing such instances of market failure – although this constitutes only one reason for supporting public service broadcasting, as Chapter 5 shows.

Neoclassical economics emerged in the 1870s, and became dominant – albeit with a range of dissenting voices around it – in the 20th century. Philosophers have observed that the rise of neoclassicism was associated with an uncoupling of economics as a discipline from fields such as history, politics and social philosophy, as well as a downplaying of the relevance of social structure or ethical questions. In contrast to the classical economics of Adam Smith, David Ricardo and John Stuart Mill, the neoclassical approach to economic questions was increasingly based around methodological individualism, rational choice theory and quantitative methods (Reiss, 2013). Reflective of a wider 'tendency for the social sciences to mimic the natural sciences', William Jackson has observed that 'neoclassical theory...squeezed out any inkling of culture' and that 'economics was the social science least receptive to cultural thought' (Jackson, 2009, p. 44).

As the media clearly have a cultural dimension, this does render applications of neoclassical economic methods to the media problematic. Even those who apply conventional economic tools to the study of media and culture nonetheless recognise its problems and limitations. The cultural economist David Throsby has critiqued the 'intellectual imperialism' of neoclassical economics, observing that 'neoclassical economics is in fact quite restrictive in its assumptions... [and] its supremacy can be challenged if a broader view of the discourse of economics is taken' (Throsby, 2001, p. 2).

Alan Albarran (2010, pp. 20–21) distinguishes between three theoretical traditions in media economics. The first is the *neoclassical* approach, which involves the application of standard tools of microeconomics to media industries and markets. A second approach is what Albarran terms an *applied* approach, that combines elements of conventional economics with business management theories, such as theories of corporate strategy and organisational behaviour, and which is typically oriented towards advising media managers or government policy-makers. Examples of such an applied approach can be found in Albarran *et al.* (2006), Küng-Shankelman *et al.* (2008) and Picard (2011a), as well as in the *International Journal of Media Management*. Finally, there is the *critical political economy* tradition, which has drawn upon influences that have included Marxist political economy, critical institutionalism and British cultural studies, and which largely positions itself as being in opposition to the mainstream media economics tradition (Wasko, 2004; Golding and Murdock, 2005; Mosco, 2009; Hardy, 2014). The critical political economy approach will be discussed in Chapter 2.

Features of media economics

In order to capture key elements of media economics, we will identify seven core elements of media generally, and identify ways the mainstream approach deals with them:

1. The heterogeneous nature of media products;
2. Dual media markets;
3. Media industries that tend towards concentration of ownership and oligopolistic markets;
4. The structure–conduct–performance (SCP) approach to understanding media firm behaviour;
5. Social drivers of media consumer behaviour;
6. Contracts and media creative producers; and
7. Government policies towards media from the perspective of competition policy, public goods and externalities.

Heterogeneous media products

One of the recurring issues in media economics is the inability to speak of a single, homogeneous *media product*. Doyle (2013, p. 12) has observed that it is 'difficult to define what constitutes a unit of media content'. With a newspaper or magazine, for example, the overall package is the unit that is purchased, rather than individual articles or sections. By contrast, for radio and television, it is the individual programme that is the meaningful unit, rather than the station or network providing it. These lines do become blurred: subscription television is premised upon a preparedness to pay for bundles of channels, while the migration of print media online has meant that it is individual articles that are increasingly consumed rather than the whole publication.

This lack of clarity surrounding the unit of media content makes it difficult to determine the *price* of different media, since there are highly variable interpretations of what is being consumed. The content that is being priced is also typically platform-specific: books and newspapers are both forms of the written word, for instance, but they are quite different platforms for media content. The use of the generic term 'content' to describe media products can obscure important distinctions between media types. The content may be primarily focused upon providing *information* (e.g. news, documentary) or *entertainment* (e.g. comedy, drama, talent or game show). It may also be considered to have the attributes of a *cultural good*, being 'appreciated for the ways in which [it enriches] our cultural environment' (Doyle, 2013, p. 13), or it may be considered 'low culture' or 'mere' popular entertainment (noting that definitions of 'high' and 'low' culture are always contestable). Finally, media content can take the form of a discrete *product* (e.g. a feature film or a DVD), or it may be a service or platform through which content is accessed. In the case of digital media forms such as *Facebook* and *Twitter*, it is the platform itself that is the service accessed by consumers, and the content consists of what individuals choose to put on the platform or how they communicate with one another through it.

Dual media markets

The lack of clarity surrounding the price of media arising from the difficulties in defining the media product are reinforced by media markets often taking the form of *dual markets,* where many media industries operate simultaneously in the consumer market and the advertising market. Media firms are seeking to market their content to consumers through a variety of delivery platforms, for which consumers may pay money directly, give their free time or choose to subscribe to the content service provider (newspaper, TV station, website etc.). But these media firms are also participating in the *advertising* market, whereby they sell space or time to purchasers of advertising, which include corporations, small businesses, government agencies, political parties, non-government organisations and individual sellers (as with classified advertising).

In the case of advertiser-financed media, media firms 'create one product but participate in two separate good and service markets ... and that performance in each market affects performance in the other' (Picard, 1989, p. 17). Commercial media firms therefore 'sell access to audiences to advertisers' (Picard, 1989, p. 18) as a key part of their business. Not all media participate in the advertising market: publicly funded media organisations are often required not to carry commercial advertising, and many media industries, such as the book industry, are based exclusively upon direct sales to consumers. But for those who do, the two markets are integrally linked: evidence of attracting large audiences or readerships enables media businesses to charge higher rates for advertising, and the ability to attract advertising becomes a significant – perhaps the most significant – driver of decisions related to media content.

Concentrated media industries

In contrast to the potentially boundless nature of media products, there has typically been a clearer definition of what constitute media industries. A characteristic listing of media industries would make reference to newspapers and magazines, other print and publishing industries (e.g. book publishing), film, radio, television, advertising and music. It is highly unusual for a media industry to approximate the conditions for perfect competition. More typically, media industries have significant concentration of ownership, and market structures are characterised by a spectrum of market structures between perfect competition and pure monopoly, including *oligopoly* (few sellers, limited or no price competition) and *monopolistic competition* (more sellers than oligopoly, and a mix of product and price competition) (Table 1.1).

In their assessment of the degree of competition in US media markets in the mid-1990s, Albarran and Dimmick (1996) found no media industry to be perfectly competitive. They identified the book, magazine, newspaper and radio industries as being characterised by monopolistic competition, and the television (broadcast and cable), film and music recording industries as oligopolistic. In more recent times, the market for websites has approximated perfect competition, as no single provider has a natural advantage that they can capitalise upon, although the market for web search is clearly closer to monopolistic competition, dominated by Microsoft, Google, Apple and Firefox, and the apps market is an oligopoly, dominated by Google, Apple and – to a lesser degree – Microsoft.

The most commonly used measures of media concentration have been the *concentration ratio (CR)* and the *Hirschman-Herfindahl Index*

Table 1.1 Spectrum of competition across market structures

Type of market structure	Characteristics	Media industry examples	Concentration ratio (CR)
Perfect competition	Multiple sellers Homogeneous product Easy substitution of product Strong price competition	Websites	$CR_n \leq 1\%$
Monopolistic competition	Few sellers Product differentiation Mix of product and price competition	Book publishing Magazines Radio National newspapers	$CR4 \leq 33\%$
Oligopoly	Few sellers Similar product Non-price competition Competition for market share Tendency towards collusion	Music recording Film Television Web search Apps Telecommunications	$CR4 \geq 50\%$
Monopoly	Single seller Homogeneous product		$CR1 = 100\%$

Source: Derived from Albarran (2010, pp. 53–54).

(*HHI*). The CR identifies the market share in an industry that is held by the top four firms (CR4) and the top eight firms (CR8). As a general rule, an industry is considered to be highly concentrated if CR4 $\geq$ 50% (CR8 $\geq$ 75%), moderately concentrated if CR4 = 34–49% (CR8 = 51–74%) and lowly concentrated if CR4 $\leq$ 33% (CR8 $\leq$ 50%). One weakness of the concentration ratio is that it tells us little about size disparities among the top four or top eight firms that may impact upon how they compete with one another. The HHI is sensitive to these disparities. It is the sum of the squared market share, expressed as a percentage, of all firms in an industry. HHI has a maximum value of 10,000 for a monopoly (100^2) and approaches zero if an industry is highly competitive (it would equal $1^2 = 1$, for instance, if an industry had 100 firms who all had 1% market share). The rule of thumb with the HHI is that there is high concentration if HHI > 1800, low concentration if HHI < 1000 and moderate concentration for the range in between. One drawback of HHI is that it requires knowledge of the market shares of all firms, and since it tends to correlate with CRs at any rate, most media economists consider calculation of CR to be sufficient (Hoskins *et al.*, 2004, pp. 146–47).

In explaining why media industries are particularly prone to market concentration, economies of scale and scope play an important role. *Economies of scale* exist where 'the cost of providing an extra unit of a good falls as the scale of output expands' (Doyle, 2013, p. 15). Industries with complex technological requirements, and the need for high upfront investments of fixed capital to begin production (what are referred to as sunk costs), tend to experience significant economies of scale. In the case of media industries, such 'bigger is better' tendencies are accentuated by *public good* elements of the product, which make marginal costs of reaching new consumers very low relative to the costs of entry for potential new competitors. *Economies of scope* refer to the capacity to make savings and gain efficiencies by using the same inputs to produce more than one good or service, or being able to repackage or repurpose the same product in order to be sold in other markets. Economies of scope are very important to media industries as content is very fungible: games can be repurposed as films, and films as games; television programmes can be repackaged as DVD box sets; musical performers can record their concerts and sell them as live albums and DVDs; and so on.

Media concentration is likely to have negative consequences for overall media performance, as measured in terms of productive efficiency and technological innovation. Media concentration can also promote rent seeking, or the acquisition of valuable rights through political lobbying, by suppressing competition and the emergence of lower-cost alternatives. Finally, media concentration may also restrict cultural and information diversity, thereby restricting the diversity of views and opinions available to citizens, and thus impairing the operations of a democratic polity (Picard, 2011b; Freedman, 2014). At the same time, governments may accept oligopolistic market structures as a condition for other quid pro quos, such as requirements to reinvest high corporate profits so as to ensure other social or cultural policy goals including the provision of services to smaller markets, the provision of less profitable forms of media content such as locally produced drama and children's programming and the provision of local news services (Flew, 2006).

Governments may also take the view that they require large domestic media companies who can be 'national champions' in highly competitive international markets (Picard, 2011b, p. 360). As a general rule, collusion among businesses is more possible when the nature of a product and the demand for it is relatively stable, and is harder to maintain in conditions where products are becoming increasingly complex and differentiated, or where new technologies are changing the nature of access to the product (Hoskins *et al.*, 2004, p. 195).

Media firm behaviour: The SCP model

The significance of industry concentration ratios lies in their capacity to predict the conduct of *media firms*. According to the *structure-conduct-performance* (SCP) or *industrial organisation* (IO) model, industry structure shapes market conduct and firm behaviour. Market structures are shaped not only by the concentration of control in a media industry but also by the scope to apply barriers to entry to restrict potential new competitors. This will in turn shape the conduct of firms, as measured by such variables as pricing policies, product differentiation, advertising behaviour and the willingness to innovate in the development of new technologies. Douglas Gomery observed that 'economic theory has a hard time with oligopolists' (Gomery, 1989, p. 50), because they have a wide range of behavioural choices not dictated by market pressures. Individual firms in an oligopoly possess incentives both to cooperate and to compete with one another. For example, they will compete vigorously for market share and advertising revenues, but will generally be reluctant to lower prices, as this can have the effect of reducing the profitability of all firms in the industry (as has occurred, for instance, with the airline industry worldwide). They also have incentives to maintain barriers to entry for potential new competitors into their industry, whether through acting to slow the development of new technologies that may threaten their business models or by lobbying politicians to create or maintain restrictions on market entry.

Media businesses have also been particularly likely to develop as *conglomerates*, operating across multiple industries and markets. Dimmick (2006, p. 357) has argued that 'the media firm that produces a single product in a single market is largely a relic of the 19th century... the contemporary media landscape... is dominated by firms that operate in multiple markets, selling multiple products on an international scale'. A key aim of conglomeration strategies is to achieve cross-media *synergies* 'by retooling content for additional uses, by trying to create successful cross-media concept products in film, books, and games, and by using staff from one media operation to provide services to another' (Picard, 2011b, p. 212). Where successful, such synergies can be very powerful. Disney is perhaps the most famous case study in achieving synergies across its films, television programmes, books, theme parks and consumer products, all of which mutually reinforce particular strengths of the Disney brand (entertainment focus, orientation to families, politically non-contentious product, etc.). But while many focus on the upsides of conglomerate synergies and the success of Disney's 'house of brands' (Murray, 2005) strategy, the history of media mergers and takeovers also reveals many failures arising from loss of focus within the combined entity, incompatibility between corporate cultures, the downgrading of skills relevant to a particular industry and loss of dynamism in the merged entity. The oft-mentioned media case of such failure is the AOL-Time Warner merger.

Media consumers

Media economics follows the main aspects of *consumer behaviour* derived from neoclassical economics and applies them to media markets. These include the assumption that the level of personal satisfaction derived from additional consumption of a good or service declines over time (*law of diminishing marginal utility*) and that consumers respond positively to a fall in price (i.e. consume more) and negatively to a price increase (i.e. consume less). How responsive consumers are to such price changes determines the downward slope of the demand curve, and hence how producers are affected (*price elasticity of demand*). The demand for particular goods and services is also influenced by changes in price for other goods and services, whether they are direct substitutes (e.g. laptop, desktop and tablet computers), or complementary (e.g. Apple iPhones and apps from the iTunes store): this is known as the *cross-elasticity of demand*.

Some goods and services are also subject to greater increases in demand as incomes rise, as measured by the *income elasticity of demand*. What is known as 'Engel's Law' (after the 19th-century German economist Ernst Engel) predicts that there is a proportionately greater increase in the demand for cultural goods and services as incomes rise, as barriers to participation in cultural activities are reduced, and people are less subject to the iron necessities of economic subsistence. As a result of enhanced economic prosperity, people are more able to pursue what the psychologist Abraham Maslow referred to as 'higher-order needs', which include greater opportunities to appreciate culture in its various forms (Zweimuller, 2000).

A general limitation of neoclassical consumer economics is its uncoupling of individual demand preferences from the wider social and cultural context in which individual consumption decisions are made. This method is known as *methodological individualism* and will be discussed in more detail below, but the difficulties in uncoupling individual choices from society-wide influences were noted by economists such as Harvey Leibenstein. Leibenstein (1950) famously identified three 'effects' arising from social influences on individual consumption preferences that ran counter to the basic underlying assumption of neoclassical theory that 'the consumption behaviour of any individual is independent of the consumption of others' (Leibenstein, 1950, p. 184). The three cases that Leibenstein examined were: (a) *bandwagon effects*, where individuals want to 'wear, buy, do, consume, and behave like their fellows, in order to "join the crowd, be one of the boys," etc.' (Leibenstein, 1950, p. 184); (b) *snob effects*, where individuals pursue exclusiveness through 'the purchase of distinctive clothing, foods, houses, or anything else that individuals may believe will in some way set them off from the mass of mankind' (Leibenstein, 1950, p. 184); and (c) *Veblen effects*, named after the late 19th-century economist Thorstein Veblen, and referring to forms of 'conspicuous consumption', where the decision to purchase particular goods and services is positively related to the price of a good or service, that is the more expensive an item is, the more it is desired.

Contracts and creative media producers

A key feature of the media industries is that, in medium- to large-scale enterprises, the firms are not themselves producers of most of the content that they make available to consumers. Rather, they are typically aggregators, organisers and distributors of content that is *produced under contract by creative workers*, whether as individuals or small groups (as is characteristically the case with music and publishing), or as small production houses (as with television broadcasting). While the precise nature of the relationship varies between forms, across industries and over time, it is a characteristic of the creative industries that 'creative' and 'management' functions are structurally separate, with large-scale bureaucracy typically providing a poor 'fit' for creative cultural production (Davis and Scase, 2000).

The economist Richard Caves has observed that contracts between creative workers and institutions are a pervasive feature of the media and creative industries. Caves argues that the pervasiveness of contracts arises at one level from the complexities of cultural production, since 'complex projects require the collaboration of several parties, each providing different but complementary inputs or resources' (Caves, 2000, p. 12). There is also considerable risk and uncertainty around both the delivery of final cultural products on time and the likely market success of the final product, or 'the prospective buyers' valuation of the project's output' (Caves, 2000, p. 13). Reputation plays an important role in these industries, and it is one factor generating differences in salaries and contracts among people with comparable skills. Caves proposes that in the media and creative industries 'the firm can be regarded as a nexus of contracts' (Caves, 2000, p. 15), and his argument will be considered in more detail in Chapter 3.

Economics of media policy

Media economics has long been engaged with public policy questions (Doyle, 2006), and the influence of economic approaches to media and communications policy has increased around the world over recent decades (van Cuilenberg and McQuail, 2003). Writing in the early 1990s, Entman and Wildman (1992, p. 5) observed that 'policy researchers seem to divide roughly between ... the "market economics" and "social value" schools of thought, and the two are often so far apart in their assumptions and languages that they are unable to communicate with each other'. They observed that the 'market economics' approach had been highly influential in communications policy-making, and that its core assumption was 'that communications policy issues can be analysed most fruitfully as problems in maximising economic efficiency ... [and] that economic efficiency would promote other desirable goals' (Entman and Wildman, 1992, p. 7). The key challenge for media reformers, as they saw it, was to know how to speak the language of market economics, in order to better present arguments grounded in 'social value' norms and assumptions.

Media economics may be applied to policy questions whose focus is not primarily economic in nature. For example, the promotion of diversity and media pluralism is often identified as a media policy goal, in order 'to ensure access to a variety of information sources, opinions, and expression so that individuals can form their own views and be well represented in the media' (Picard, 2011b, p. 361). Given such a normative policy goal, media economics can be applied to identify the most cost-effective means of achieving it, by assessing policy responses such as subsidies to media producers, investment in public service media or promotion of greater competition in media markets. Similarly, governments may see a role for media in promoting a distinctive national culture, and different policy responses can be assessed on a cost-benefit basis, such as subsidies to local producers, investment in nationally based media or quotas that set limits to imported content (Grant, 2011).

Media economics also identifies specific instances where government intervention is considered a necessary response to *market failure*. Three areas are most commonly discussed in this regard. The first is that of concentration of ownership, and the implications of media industries tending towards monopoly or oligopoly. Even where a 'marketplace of ideas' understanding of the primary role of media policy prevails, the concentration of ownership is seen as undesirable in forcing up prices, restricting entry to potential new competitors and producing disincentives to innovation, as well as potentially giving too much political power to 'media moguls'. Economists typically recommend that governments structure media policy in ways that minimise the extent of media concentration where possible.

Second, there are *externalities*, or costs and benefits borne by parties other than those directly engaged in producing or consuming the good or service in question. Externalities may be negative or positive: excessive violence in the media may be seen to generate negative externalities by promoting anti-social behaviour, whereas locally produced media content may promote positive externalities such as citizens' better understanding their national culture, or encouraging overseas travellers to visit the country. Policies such as content standards regulations or local content rules may provide ways of minimising negative externalities or promoting positive ones in such instances.

Finally, there is the case of *public goods*, or goods and services that are: (1) non-rivalrous, in that one person's consumption does not prevent another person from consuming the same good; and (2) non-excludable, where price-based discrimination between consumers would not be appropriate. Both broadcast media and Internet-based content have had these public good elements, where it is suggested that private provision may lead to undersupply relative to the socially optimal level of provision. Government support for non-profit public service broadcasters (PSBs) such as the BBC in the United Kingdom, the CBC in Canada, NHK in Japan, the ABC in Australia and many others worldwide is often justified on such criteria. PSBs are often required by legislative mandate to provide programme types that would be undersupplied by commercial media and which are considered to have cultural value or merit good attributes, such as children's programming, documentaries, arts and science programmes and programmes for cultural and linguistic minorities. Public broadcasting can be considered as a government response to both the public good nature of broadcasting, guaranteeing free access to over-the-air media content to all of their citizens and to the allocation of resources between programme types found in commercial broadcasting, by ensuring the supply of programming they perceive as most likely to result in positive externalities.

Debating media economics

Mainstream media economics has been subject to various critiques from communications, media and cultural studies researchers, who typically discount its ability to provide insights into the operations of media industries. For critical political economists such as Wasko *et al.* (2011, p. 4), media economics 'avoids political and historical analysis... [and] mostly accepts the status quo'. Vincent Mosco has contended that neoclassical economics was a 'hollow science' that 'seeks to comprehend economic behaviour without understanding the complexities of power, social structure, organizational behaviour, and cultural practice' (Mosco, 2009, p. 62). In doing so, he noted the earlier critique by sociologists Daniel Bell and Irving Kristol, who argued that economists thought that 'the only reality worth examining is what is observable, measurable, and quantifiable' (quoted in Mosco, 2009, p. 63).

Such critiques echo criticisms of mainstream neoclassical economics that have been made by other economists. Stilwell (2002, p. 3) argued that 'models of market exchange under competitive conditions fail to illuminate the world in which we live', while Keen (2001, p. 4) argued that 'virtually every aspect of conventional economic theory is intellectually unsound'. The Global Financial Crisis (GFC) of 2008, whose depth and severity took most economists and policy-makers by surprise, acted as a catalyst for further critiques of economics as a discipline. Quiggin attacked the 'zombie ideas' that continued to influence economic policy, and called on the economics profession to 'produce a more realistic, humble, and above all socially useful body of thought' (Quiggin, 2010, p. 211). The Nobel Prize winning economist Joseph Stiglitz said that economists were culpable in the events that led up to the GFC as many were 'so blinded by their faith in free markets that they couldn't see the problems it was creating. Economists had moved... from being a scientific discipline into becoming free market capitalism's biggest cheerleader' (Stiglitz, 2010, p. 238). The University of Chicago legal theorist and economist Richard Posner argued that the GFC arose in part from 'the persistence of theories that did not yield good predictions...due to the absence of competing theories that could be fitted to the type of models with which modern economists were comfortable' (Posner, 2010, p. 272).

In some instances, a critique of neoclassical economics is bound up with a more general opposition to the capitalist economic system, where mainstream economics is seen as providing intellectual justification for existing power relations, as a modern variant of what Karl Marx termed 'vulgar economy' (Bharadwaj, 1990). But in other instances, the critique of neoclassical economics as analytical method is not synonymous with rejection of the capitalist market economy. Posner, Bell and Kristol, for example, would all be seen as broadly supportive of the capitalist economic system, while Stiglitz was a former chief economist with the World Bank and an advisor to US President Bill Clinton.

There are at least three layers to the critique of mainstream economics in general, and media economics in particular. First, there is the view that it is empirically wrong in key assumptions it makes about the nature and operation of media markets. Second, it is argued that neoclassical economic theory is fundamentally flawed from a methodological point of view, due to its focus on rational choice, methodological individualism and static equilibrium states. Third, the critique that mainstream economics lacks ethical foundations arises from the absence of interdisciplinary insights from the humanities and other fields in the social sciences. At its strongest, as found in the critique of neoliberalism, neoclassical economics is seen as largely constituting a form of ideological cover to support and protect dominant political-economic interests and give intellectual credibility to attacks on trade unions, public ownership and the welfare state (Harvey, 2005).

In the remainder of this chapter, we wish to acknowledge the critiques that have been made about neoclassical economics, which lies at the core of mainstream media economics. In particular, neoclassical theories struggle with issues presented by: the existence of large corporations that can exercise differing degrees of market power; the assumptions around rational choice, methodological individualism and static equilibrium theorising; and the difficulties in recognising the contributions of other academic disciplines, notably in relation to the study of culture and institutions. It will be noted that such criticisms are not applicable across the board to the economics discipline, and that there exist very lively alternative perspectives to neoclassical theory within economics, as we discuss in this book. In subsequent chapters of this book, we discuss extensions of economics into questions that have been considered more 'cultural' than 'economic', such as the non-monetary value that citizens place upon core cultural institutions.

At the same time, while we have not come to praise mainstream economics, we have also not come to bury it. We argue in this chapter that there are many instances where conventional media economics provides important insights into important phenomena in media industries and markets. Examples discussed in this chapter include trends in the concentration of media ownership, how established media firms have been responding to the challenges of new media and digital distribution and the dynamics of product-based competition in digital media industries. In doing so, we also wish to turn the critical gaze onto critics of mainstream media economics. We also argue that many critics erroneously assume that economics is a relatively static and intellectually homogeneous discipline, that it is morally wrong to address cultural questions from an economic perspective and that economics functions largely as an ideological tool for powerful interests rather than as a set of analytical categories for making sense of the world. Our intention is to provide a more balanced account of both the insights and the limitations of mainstream neoclassical economics as applied to media industries and markets.

Empirical questions

One of the criticisms commonly made of mainstream economics is that it is overly abstract and fails to understand the dynamics of 'real world' businesses. In media economics, this is reflective of the distinction made between the applied field of media management and the more theoretical work found in media economics. But the criticism extends further, with the argument that neoclassical approaches are only applicable to highly competitive markets where all firms are price takers and none can exercise market power. To the degree that firms can become sufficiently large and powerful to control key aspects of their external environment, such as prices and product demand, neoclassical theory is assumed to become less relevant.

This argument somewhat caricatures the core claims being made in mainstream media economics, since it is generally acknowledged that almost all media markets are under conditions of oligopoly and monopolistic competition, as was noted earlier. The core proposition of mainstream media economics is the less strong one that, all other things being equal, more competition in a market can be expected to bring down prices and/or lead to changes in the product or service being offered, and that this will be of benefit to consumers. We considered this in the case of tablet PCs, where the emergence of competitors to Apple's iPad saw prices fall as the number of product suppliers increased. The corollary is, of course, that greater concentration of media ownership is likely to leave consumers worse off, which is an important reason why measures to restrict concentration of ownership are considered to be an important element of media policy. But neoclassical economics does not necessarily see ownership concentration and market competition as incompatible.

Is the concentration of media ownership increasing over time?

A key point of contention between mainstream media economists and political economists has been over whether the concentration of media ownership has been increasing or decreasing over time. The political economy perspective has drawn attention to the rise of media conglomerates and argued that ownership concentration has increased over time, to the point where it now threatens the effective functioning of liberal democracies (McChesney, 2013). By contrast, some media economists (e.g. Compaine, 2001, 2005; Thierer and Eskelsen, 2008) have argued that key media markets such as broadcasting have become more competitive since the 1980s and that the Internet and media convergence have introduced new forms of competition that threaten the traditional media giants. As Compaine (2001) put it, 'the marketplace of ideas...may be flawed, but it is getting better, not worse'.

In his comprehensive overview of media ownership trends in the United States, media economist Eli Noam (2009) used the HHI index that we outlined earlier to find that the 'digital optimists' were right to perceive that concentration was less pronounced in 2005 than it was in 1984, and that the Internet was an important part of that trend. At the same time, the 'digital pessimists' have also been right to observe an increase in media concentration between 1996 and 2005. Noam found that a key issue in understanding contemporary media ownership questions was that a two-tier media system has been evolving, with large *integrator* firms such as Apple, Google, Microsoft and others being surrounded by a large number of specialist firms

(Continued)

that undertake much of the actual content production (Noam, 2009, pp. 436–37). This has weakened the power of the traditional media giants such as Time Warner, Disney, News Corporation, Viacom/CBS and Sony, as their challengers are increasingly big ICT and software companies rather than those more traditionally associated with industries such as film, broadcasting, music or publishing.

Noam cautions against assuming that this means a more competitive media environment, as network effects are very powerful in the new media businesses. For instance, companies such as Apple and Google have now become important gatekeepers for the digital distribution of content, particularly with the rise of an 'apps' environment that is more 'curated' than the World Wide Web. It also means that power relations within media industries have been shifting, with the digital distribution platforms gaining in market power relative to the traditional content producing copyright-based industries.

Noam's work draws attention to the extent to which the period from about 2005 onwards was one of perceived crisis for many of the media conglomerates that had dominated the previous decade. Media giants such as Time Warner, Disney, News Corporation, Viacom/CBS and Sony now deal with the challenges of convergence, the migration of audiences to new platforms and the challenge of the ICT-based entities such as Google, Apple, Microsoft, Netflix, Amazon and others, as we will discuss in Chapter 5. It also raises the important point that what we understand to be a 'media industry' is not static in its nature, but is shifting and evolving over time, particularly in the context of media convergence.

Media companies are often high-profile businesses, and there is considerable public interest in the character of media owners. Media moguls such as Rupert Murdoch and Silvio Berlusconi attract worldwide attention as they merge political interests with business interests. Large corporate mergers and the existence of media conglomerates are often cited as evidence of the untrammelled power of the corporate media giants (e.g. Shah, 2009). But media economics indicates the need to look beyond size itself as an indicator of market dominance. It is pointed out that while the all-powerful media mogul is clearly a figure who attracts great public attention, he (and it is nearly always a he) is of declining significance overall, as the separation of ownership and control and the rise of institutional investors see media following other sectors towards more impersonal forms of corporate ownership. As Eli Noam points out, the largest investors in global media are rather less colourful entities such as State Street Global Advisors, Fidelity Management and Barclays Bank (Noam, 2009, p. 6). This cautionary note about the focus of critical media studies on the power of the media mogul also needs a greater awareness that, where such moguls continue to exercise power over media assets, their influence is very often a problem for the media businesses themselves, as their personal preferences may override a more clear-headed analysis of where company resources should be most profitably invested (Knee *et al.*, 2009).

Moreover, mergers and conglomeration strategies in the media industries very often fail. One problem with mergers and acquisitions is that they often bring together companies with different corporate cultures and traditions, and these mix poorly in the merged entity. The merger of Internet service provider America Online (AOL) and media giant Time Warner in 2001 was the largest corporate merger in history when it took place in 2001, but a decade later the merger had been abandoned as a failure. When News Corporation took over social media site MySpace in 2005 for $US580 million, it was heralded at the time as evidence of Rupert Murdoch 'getting' new media; when it was sold by News Corporation in 2011 for $US35 million with a dramatically diminished user base, Murdoch himself conceded that the venture had been a huge mistake.

There is also a need to avoid conflating the size of corporate entities with their control over markets. In a period of rapid technological change, as has been occurring in the global media industries over the last two decades, reductions in barriers to entry and the emergence of new products and services challenge many of the structural conditions that enable incumbent media businesses to maintain barriers to new competitors. Processes of media convergence and the transition of media content from analogue to digital formats have led to major transformations of media industries and markets worldwide. Two instances where the traditional assumptions of media economics are challenged include: the concept of scarcity and its relationship to price, as digital content is abundant and often freely available to consumers; and the understanding of an industry, as convergent media product/service providers such as Apple and Google serve as content aggregators rather than direct producers/distributors of media content (Noam, 2009).

Media economics and digital platforms

There exists a significant literature on media economics as it applies to the digital environment (e.g. Shapiro and Varian, 1999; Madden and Cooper, 2009; George and Hogendorn, 2012; Quiggin, 2013). One important issue raised is the question of network effects, where there is significant first-mover advantage to develop a new social media service as others feel compelled to join that service to maximise contact with others (as with Facebook, for example). Another is the issue of *lock-in*, where both consumers and other suppliers feel compelled to work with the established firms in order to have the most compatible software and devices, which sets limits to new competitors entering the market. Microsoft has benefited from such lock-in effects in the business software market, and Apple and Google derive such benefits in relation to the corporate strategies of apps developers for mobile phones and tablet PCs.

Steirer (2014) has argued that neoclassical principles continue to be applicable in the context of digital transformations of media industries and markets for understanding both new media players and how traditional media industries and firms are responding. He has applied neoclassical economics to digital distribution and the question of how the big Hollywood studios have been responding to the challenges of video-on-demand (VOD). Using the UltraViolet entertainment system as a case study, where consumers could acquire from DVD retailers a 'digital rights token' enabling their films to play on a variety of compatible devices and services, Steirer argued that such an initiative can be understood through the application of two neoclassical economic principles.

The first is the principle of *substitutable goods*. Consumers make decisions about how to allocate shares of their total income and/or time to home entertainment, and that entertainment can be acquired by a variety of mutually substitutable means, including DVD purchases, transactional VOD (e.g. Apple's iTunes) and VOD subscriptions (e.g. Netflix). For the Hollywood majors, the shift from DVDs to other platforms has been associated with the relative decline of their highly profitable DVD sales business to VOD services. UltraViolet was an attempt to extend the DVD sales market by enabling its products to be played on digital and mobile devices and its failure was related in part to difficulties for consumers in using the system, as compared with the ease of acquiring content through services such as iTunes or Netflix.

(Continued)

Second, the principle of *switching costs* indicates why the Hollywood majors sought to intervene in the retail space, rather than simply accepting that their products were now being acquired through digital distribution services. One of Apple's major achievements has been to ensure a degree of consumer lock-in to its combination of hardware, software and operating systems, so that the interoperability of devices and their ease of use for consumers is matched by high switching costs for moving away from Apple devices, such as the difficulties in getting products purchased on iTunes to operate on non-Apple devices. In contrast to the high sales margins on retail DVDs, the profits offered to the Hollywood majors through sales on Apple iTunes are considerably lower, so the UltraViolet initiative was in part a response to the growing market power of Apple in home entertainment.

Steirer's wider point is that critiques of neoclassical economics often miss the point that while it is not a fully sufficient means of understanding digital distribution, it is nonetheless 'essential for understanding both how specific digital distribution systems are designed to work and why these systems succeed or fail' (Steirer, 2014, p. 11). Echoing Doyle's (2013, p. 1) point about one reason for studying conventional media economics being its utility for media industry players in understanding their own competitive environment, Steirer makes the point that neoclassical economics 'serves as the dominant engine of decision-making for investors, executives, labour leaders, competition regulators, and other powerful decision-makers. Utilising neoclassical economic principles can thus assist us in understanding... the decision-making processes of businesses themselves' (Steirer, 2014, p. 12).

Methodological questions

Neoclassical microeconomics was formed around a variety of contributions to economic theory made between the 1870s and 1920s, with Alfred Marshall's 1890 text *Principles of Economics* being a key marker of the field. The five key methodological foundations of neoclassical economics (Ekelund and Hébert, 2002; Stilwell, 2002, pp. 148–54; Wildman, 2006) are:

1. *Methodological individualism*: economics is focused on how individuals derive personal pleasures or benefits (utility) from the consumption of various products and services. They do so in circumstances where each individual's utility is unique, and there is no common metric for comparing the utilities of different individuals or judging whether one person's wants are more socially worthy than another's.
2. *Marginalism*: consumers are assumed to maximise utility and firms to maximise profits, and neoclassical economics is interested in the incremental changes (changes at the margins) made to pursue such goals in response to changing relative price signals.
3. *Stable preferences*: individual tastes and preferences are taken as stable and given at any point in time, and determined independently of the behaviour of producers.
4. *Static optimisation*: the processes of utility and profit maximisation are modelled as taking place in environments where other critical factors (e.g. incomes and the general price level, prices of inputs, the state of technology, consumer demand, the behaviour of competitors in a market) are assumed to be constant when assessing the impact of one change, such as a change in relative prices.
5. *Rational actors*: neoclassical economics describes these maximising agents as rational actors, who make choices given the resources available to them to attain the combination for which utility or profit is greatest. Moreover, they do so with full information about the consequences of various alternatives, so as to make the objectively best decisions.

These are a highly restrictive set of analytical assumptions, and few would defend them as adequate descriptors of the real world. Instead, those who use such a framework argue that 'these assumptions produce more than adequate approximations to the behaviour of the real economic agents they study and that the gains in academic tractability achieved more than compensate for whatever sacrifices are made in realism of description' (Wildman, 2006, p. 72). The question has long been how much of the analytical edifice of neoclassical economic survives as its core assumptions are progressively relaxed. In the case of media economics, the fact that most media markets are oligopolistic means that the relationship between pricing behaviour and profit maximisation is considerably more uncertain and open-ended than can be assumed with markets that approximate the conditions of perfect competition.

There are many critiques of rational choice theory, in terms of its assumptions about the optimal behaviour of individuals, the rationality of beliefs and the availability of relevant information to decision-makers. Elster (2007) identified no less than 18 instances where the choices that individuals make in the real world violate canonical principles of rational choice theory. He argued that even on the most generous interpretation that rationality – rather than desires or emotions – constitutes the primary driver of human behaviour, it still needs to be acknowledged that rational choice theory rests upon subjective interpretations by individuals of what is in their best interests, and that 'the *rationality* of beliefs is a completely different matter from that of their *truth*' (Elster, 2007, p. 211).

One of the risks for those critiquing economics from outside of the discipline is that of conflating the conceptual orthodoxy that exists in undergraduate textbooks with the state-of-the-art thinking in the wider field, as found in the leading scholarly journals and among those who win the Nobel Prize for Economics. Colander *et al.* observe that the leading work in economics is no longer holding to the 'holy trinity [of] rationality, selfishness, and equilibrium', even if such ideas remain central to mainstream economics textbooks (Colander *et al.*, 2004, p. 485). They argue that this arises from the economics discipline being a large and complex system, where there is a significant time lag between the work that is occurring at the 'edges' of the discipline – work associated with evolutionary economics' complex adaptive systems or the new institutional economics, for example – and what is taught in large undergraduate programmes.

This argument suggests that we need to be wary of simply conflating the terms 'mainstream economics', 'orthodox economics', 'neoclassical economics' and economics as a whole. The 'mainstream' may well be moving away from the strictly neoclassical approach, and it is certainly the case that 'mainstream economics' has long co-existed with dissenting strands of thought within the discipline. It is also apparent that 'a large part of the mainstream profession disagrees with important dimensions of what is thought of as orthodox' (Colander *et al.*, 2004, p. 491). Insofar as the leading-edge work in the discipline is occurring outside of its core, it may also take some time to permeate outwards to the sub-disciplines in the field such as media economics.[1]

Individual agency and structural power

One reason why rational choice theory remains a part of the economics field is that it is tied to methodological individualism, which proposes that 'in the social sciences, a satisfactory explanation must ultimately be anchored in hypotheses about human behaviour' (Elster, 2007, p. 36). It 'emphasises the human agent over social structure... [and] the role of individual intentions in the explanation of social phenomena' (Hodgson, 2004, p. 16). The commitment to methodological individualism, rational choice and mathematical techniques clearly marked itself off from disciplines such as sociology, political science, history and communications, where structuralism, interpretative methods and qualitative research became more common (Ingham, 1996; Jackson, 2009). Moreover, other social sciences disciplines have not had the same commitment to an orthodox position that defines the field as economics has come to have with the neoclassical approach (Jackson, 2009, pp. 69–70).

Methodological individualism has tended to be an obstacle to economists interacting productively with other academic disciplines. It works with a strong assumption that 'individuals (intentionally or unintentionally) form society through their combined actions' (Hodgson, 2004, p. 18), whereas virtually all other social sciences view the relationship between individual agency and social institutions as a reciprocal one. In contrast to methodological individualism, a more interdisciplinary perspective allows questions of *economic power* to be given more consideration. John Kenneth Galbraith argued that 'the decisive weakness in neoclassical economics... [was] in the assumptions by which it elides the problem of power... in eliding power – in making economics a non-political subject – neoclassical theory, by the same process, destroys its relation with the real world' (Galbraith, 1973, p. 2).

The methodological individualism of mainstream economics, combined with its relative lack of attention to questions of power and politics, has also informed the critique of media economics as lacking ethical underpinnings. Golding and Murdock (2005, p. 65) distinguish political economy from mainstream media economics on the grounds that 'arguments... on the proper balance between public and private enterprise are never simply technical... [but] are always underpinned by distinctive visions of what constitutes the "public good"'. The ethical critique of media economics and the critique of methodological individualism and its neglect of questions of structural power tend to be linked. For example, we have noted that media economics provides a methodology for determining the degree of concentration of ownership in media markets, from which can be gauged a measure of whether such concentration has adverse impacts on such industries and markets. Freedman (2014) has argued that concerns about concentrated media ownership are never simply economic ones, as its influence on the quality of information and debate in democratic societies, its impact on the diversity of forms of cultural representation and its influence on the employment opportunities for creative workers are all factors that are not captured through media ownership metrics. It is thus argued that these are ethical questions that have a political and policy overlay, to which media economics can only provide one form of input.

Conclusion

In this chapter, we have sought to neither praise nor bury mainstream media economics. Rather, we have approached media economics as an analytical method, with some core principles based around the theory of supply and demand as applied to media products and services. These include: the diverse forms that the 'media product' takes; the concept of media markets as dual product markets, servicing both advertisers and audiences; the metrics used to measure media concentration; features of oligopolistic media markets and media conglomerates; assumptions about both consumers and producers of media content; and applications of media economics to media policy, with particular reference to market failure, externalities and public goods.

It was noted that mainstream media economics, as derived from neoclassical economic theory, is widely critiqued by more critically minded media, communications and cultural studies theorists, echoing critiques from within the economic profession. In the case of some elements of the theory, such as methodological individualism and a tendency to lack openness to the insights from other disciplines, such criticisms would appear to be warranted. But we would reject attempts to then consign mainstream media economics to the analytical dustbin, as can happen in the media, communications and cultural studies fields. It is a method best suited to the analysis of changes in particular media industries and markets, the relationship between changes in price and other variables (e.g. new products and services arising from new technologies), and corporate behaviour in environments characterised by differing degrees of competition. Understood in this way, it continues to have relevance to the analysis of convergent digital media as well as the more traditional media industries. It was also noted that caution needs to be exercised in critiquing the economics discipline from outside, as it is possible to underestimate both the degree of diversity and heterogeneity within the field and the extent to which work at the leading edges of economic theory differs from some of the more prosaic assumptions of textbook versions of both mainstream media economics and economics more generally.

2 Critical Political Economy of the Media

The critical political economy of the media approach is an extension of the general study of political economy that draws on 18th-century Scottish Enlightenment thinking and subsequent 19th-century Marxist critiques, emphasising therefore notions of capital, class, contradiction, conflict and oppositional struggles. In his major study of the field, Vincent Mosco (2009) defines political economy as the 'study of the social relations, particularly the power relations, that mutually constitute the production, distribution, and consumption of resources, including communication resources' (p. 24). Mosco traces the early development of the field and tradition in the United States to the work of Dallas Smythe and Herbert Schiller, both of whom attributed their political and intellectual development to personal observations and experiences of the radical transformation in American and global politics during the first half of the 20th century, particularly the political and cultural legacies of the Great Depression, the rise of Fascism and antifascism and McCarthyism (Dervin, 1993; Mosco, 2009).

Recognising the importance communication played in the broader economy, Smythe sought to apply political economy in order to expose the power relations that were reproduced in media institutions, embedded in technology and represented in communications policies (Smythe, 1960, 1977, 1981), while Schiller's work offered a sustained critique of the information society, documenting strong ties between government and military and international extension of the US communication system (Schiller, 1992 [1969]), the growing transnationalisation of media corporations (Schiller, 1973), relations of dependency between Western media and the 'Third World' (Schiller, 1976), as well as the growing gaps in access to communication and the 'digital divide' arguments that follow from those gaps (Schiller, 1996).

Political economy of the media has developed into an established theoretical framework, drawing attention not only to how the media operate as businesses but also to the way in which power, class systems, structural inequalities and value operate in the increasingly complex production–distribution–consumption chain of media products. It takes as its object of study mediated communication in all of its forms and thus, while its object of study includes both the transmission of information and the social construction of meaning, it rejects the *essentialism* of either economics (the realm of structure, institution and material activity) or culture (the realm of meaning and subjectivity), arguing that both are mutually constituted out of social and cultural processes of exchange which differ but also multiply determined by shared practices (Mosco, p. 68).

In developing a model for the political economy of communication in the United Kingdom, Murdock and Golding (1973) sought to examine the processes of consolidation and concentration at work in media industries. Their early work addressed particularly the manner in which horizontal integration (takeovers and mergers of businesses within the same industry) and vertical integration (takeovers and mergers of businesses in related industries) are employed to control all stages of media production and distribution across multiple sectors, as well as the manner in which media conglomerates threaten cultural diversity and reproduce class inequalities through promoting the interests of power elites. Golding and Murdock later argued that political economy goes beyond technical issues of efficiency to engage with basic moral questions of justice, equity and the public good (2005, pp. 62–63). Nicholas Garnham (1979) connected political economy with the Frankfurt school and the modes of cultural production and consumption within capitalist societies, arguing that media had both 'a direct economic role as creators of surplus value through commodity production and exchange and an indirect role, through advertising, in the creation of surplus value within other sectors of commodity production' (1979, p. 132). Garnham's work also recognised that despite corporate and private capital controlling the means of cultural production, cultural commodities will not always necessarily support the dominant ideology.

Dwayne Winseck (2011), in arguing against a singular political economy approach, suggests that political economies of the media evolve in relation to developments in their object of analysis. The fact that the object of analysis – institutions, technologies, markets and society – have undergone and continue to undergo so much change means, for Winseck, that the scholarship of political economy itself 'must be open to theoretical revision more than ever' (2011, p. 13). In rejecting the idea that political economy 'comes in one flavour', Winseck identified four perspectives that 'have considerable currency' in the field: Neoclassical political economy; Radical media political economy; Schumpeterian institutional political economy; and, the Cultural industries school (2011, p. 3).

For Winseck, *neoclassical political economy* is 'instantly recognised by its stress on the "marketplace of ideas" in democratic societies' (2011, p. 17). While this 'neoclassical political economy', which is perhaps more accurately termed 'public choice theory', draws upon neoclassical economics as outlined in Chapter 1, it differs from mainstream neoclassicism in two key respects. First, there is a questioning of the degree to which government regulation can resolve issues of market failure, as it draws attention to issues of *government failure*. It is argued that in contrast to a 'normative' theory of regulators as serving the public interest, a 'positive' theory of regulatory conduct identifies public bureaucrats as pursuing their own self-interest as optimising economic agents (Hoskins *et al.*, 2004, pp. 303–07; Christensen, 2011). More often than not, this can lead them to form coalitions of interest with those from the industries they regulate, to the detriment of the public interest, and particularly the interests of consumers and potential new competitors (Christensen, 2011, pp. 97–100). Another feature of this variant of neoclassical economics is the view that *information scarcity is an illusion*, as Internet technologies are giving consumers a cornucopia of choice in terms of content, media distribution outlets, reception and playback devices and storage options in a process that is only being delayed by the self-interested blocking tactics of regulators and incumbent media interests (e.g. Compaine, 2005; Thierer and Eskelsen, 2008).

Winseck further divides *radical media political economy* into the *monopoly capital* and *digital capitalism* schools. Winseck associates the monopoly capital school with the scholarship of Robert McChesney, whose extensive body of work emphasises the role media play in democratic and capitalist societies, and the relationship between media, journalism and governance. This school of political economy gives great emphasis to the public good characteristics of free press journalism in a democratic tradition and argues that quality journalism will be under-produced unless it is subsidised through either advertising or public mechanisms (e.g. tax- or licence-funded public broadcasting). McChesney and Nichols' *The Death and Life of American Journalism* (2010) is exemplary of the field, arguing that the conflict between public-good journalism and the profit-generation of media industries is longstanding, that a loss of advertising revenue to the Internet caused the collapse of commercial journalism in the 2000s and that a sufficient free press in the digital age will again require massive enlightened public subsidies.

The *digital capitalism* school of radical media political economy emerges from Dan Schiller's (1999) conceptualisation of the economics of the information society and the digital networks that constitute its central organising principles that, in his view, continue to serve primarily corporate users. This branch of political economy argues that the Internet has developed as a commercial, transnational, corporate communication system to meet the needs of business, and that despite increased access for citizens, the Internet remains an overwhelmingly controlled network and media channel. In Schiller's view, media industries have always served to deepen the processes of commodification, initially through advertising or direct payment. Thus, the argument goes, the digitisation of media content, distribution, playback and storage makes the monetisation and commodification of media, audiences and information both easier and more readily available, and the consistent 'central tendency' of digital capitalism 'is to deepen and expand the capitalist market system' (Mosco, 2009, p. 120).

Schumpeterian institutional political economy differs from neoclassical and radical political economy schools in that it: (1) regards technological innovation as the motor of competition in capitalist economies, rather than price and markets; (2) holds that technological innovation creates temporary monopolies and super-profits that attract new rivals; (3) views 'creative destruction' as a central fixture of capitalism; and (4) privileges technology and economics as 'agents' of change over people and social forces. Melody (2007) argued that such an approach emphasised the manner in which new technologies introduce obsolescence for many older, established technologies, associated business models, industry structures, government policies and regulations, as well as 'a significant portion of the conventional wisdom and mainstream thinking across all the social sciences' (Melody, 2007, p. 70).

The *cultural industries* approach to political economy, as exemplified in the work of David Hesmondhalgh (2013), has always taken 'the term "industries" seriously and attempted to apply both a more detailed and nuanced Marxist economic analysis and the more mainstream industrial and information economics to the analysis of the production, distribution and consumption of symbolic forms' (Garnham, 2005, p. 18). The cultural industries approach is less concerned with direct economic power and domination by powerful elites, instead drawing attention to the persuasive and seductive 'soft power' and ideological influences of cultural industries.

For Mosco, all schools of political economic thought share four central and significant ideas:

1. The goal of understanding *historical change* and the vast social upheavals that transformed societies once based on agricultural labour into manufacturing, industrial and – of particular interest to political economy of communication – information societies;
2. An interest in the *totality of social relations*, with focus on the mutual influence and relationships the media, the political, the economic, the social and the cultural share;
3. A commitment to *moral philosophy* and to the values that create social behaviour and the principles that ought to guide efforts to change it;
4. A commitment to *social praxis* wherein intellectual life is viewed as a means of 'bringing about social change and social intervention as a means of advancing knowledge' (Mosco 2009, p. 4).

Janet Wasko (2004) outlines four main themes of inquiry framing political economy of media and communications.

First, *media/communications business* examines the transnational media companies that control media and communications systems and is founded on the assumption that a market model now dominates the media, and that communication and information are not only key components of the market but significant industries in and of themselves. Attention has been given to the privatisation of public media and the relaxation of state control of national communications infrastructure (including telecommunications infrastructure); the opening of additional commercialised global markets for media and entertainment conglomerates; the growth of global advertising and public relations; the diversification of content within and across conglomerates and the accompaniment of synergistic cross promotion and franchising; the expansion and proliferation of commercial messages across media landscape; the increasing commercialisation of new communication and information systems at the expense of universal public access; the concentration of the competitive media marketplace and the power of incumbency; and the influence of concentration on the availability of diverse and alternate views, particularly in news media.

Second, an *internationalisation and globalisation* theme that seeks to incorporate an understanding of how transnational structures of power operate, particularly in the process of transforming cultural messages into media commodities, with specific attention given to the way international and local corporate, governmental and non-governmental institutions operate to mediate global and local power.

Third, a *media-state relations* theme that examines relationships between media power and state power, as well as the media's relationships with other economic sectors, with emphasis upon the ways in which the state supports the broader media economy and media corporations, by, for example, clearing barriers to foreign markets and protecting intellectual property rights.

And fourth, a *resistance/opposition* theme that seeks to redress fundamental imbalances in global communication and power, specifically women, minority groups and labour along with the meaning of citizenship in a system that addresses people primarily as consumers.

Recurrent concerns of critical political economy include: scepticism towards markets; the dominance of large corporations and the growing commodification of culture; globalisation and the international division of communications and cultural labour; and a growing concern to develop environmental political economy as it applies to media. Additionally, a characteristic feature of critical political economy is scepticism towards the role played by markets for media and culture. This includes both scepticism towards the ability to understand the relevant industries by focusing on markets and a critical view of the impact of market values on media culture, often expressed in the 'dominant ideology' thesis. Critical political economists typically question the explanatory capacity of those forms of media and cultural economics that take the market and the forces of supply and demand as their starting point. In their book *Global Hollywood*, Miller *et al.* (2005) argue that 'the neoclassical vision of Hollywood asserts that the supposedly neutral mechanisms of market competition exchange materials at costs that ensure the most efficient people are producing, and their customers are content', but that such a model lacks realism since 'the rhythms of supply and demand, operating unfettered by states, religions, unions, superstitions and fashion, have never existed as such' (Miller *et al.*, 2005, p. 109). The bracketing off of economics from other areas of social analysis, as well as the lack of an explicit moral framework, has also generated criticism from political economists. Hesmondhalgh (2013) argued that 'neoclassical economics is not concerned with determining human needs and rights, nor with intervening in questions of social justice. Instead, it focuses on how human wants might be most efficiently satisfied'; he observed that 'such a bracketing off of questions concerning power and justice is limiting' (Hesmondhalgh, 2013, p. 38).

A second set of concerns is that, to the extent that market dynamics do in fact shape media and culture in capitalist societies, this leads, on the one hand, to greater corporate control over media and culture and, on the other, to the commodification of culture. In relation to media industries, Golding and Murdock (2005) have argued that 'media production has been increasingly commandeered by large corporations', and that corporate power has been extended in recent years through 'the sale of public assets to private investors (privatization), the introduction of competition into markets that were previously commanded by public monopolies (liberalisation), and the continuing squeeze on publicly funded cultural institutions' (Golding and Murdock, 2005, p. 64; c.f. Herman and McChesney, 1997; McChesney and Schiller, 2003; Miller et al., 2005).

'Commodification' is a term used in Marxist political economy to describe 'the process of transforming things valued for their use into marketable products that are valued for what they can bring in exchange' (Mosco, 2009, p. 127). Political economists associate the rise of corporate power and influence with the commodification of culture (Golding and Murdock, 2005, pp. 64–65; Mosco, 2009, pp. 133–43). For critical political economists, adverse consequences of the commodification of culture include:

1. Greater control over cultural production by a small number of private corporations more accountable to shareholders and financiers than to the public interest or the public good;
2. Greater corporate influence over media and cultural production through advertising and sponsorship;
3. Access to media and cultural products being increasingly dependent upon capacity to pay, thereby accentuating the cultural dimensions of social and economic inequalities;
4. The potential to reduce risk and innovation in favour of familiar and well-tested genres and formats, in order to maximize audience share;
5. The ability to use economic power to influence public debates and to exclude alternative viewpoints which dissent from the views of dominant corporate interests.

A third area of concern is an examination of the increasingly sophisticated international division of communication labour. An example here is Miller et al.'s (2005) notion of the new international division of cultural labour (NICL), with reference to Hollywood's dominance and the strategies that are used to Americanise the production, copyright, distribution, promotion and exhibition of films that use NICL to minimise cost and maximise profit. The authors tail their discussion by asserting the need to make (screen) content 'more representative, inclusive and multiple in its sources, texts and effects' while provoking 'alternative, more salutary conditions and possibilities for our own cultural labour and for our brothers and sisters in the culture works everywhere' (Miller *et al.*, 2005, p. 362).

Contemporary themes

We have devoted most time in this section on established, canonical perspectives in critical political economy. The field is constantly evolving, however, and producing new accounts that address, for example, the environmental crisis, digitisation and the Internet, non-Western media dynamics and extended attention to media corporation history. In so doing, they both exemplify the approaches identified by Wasko and Mosco and take them into new areas.

A growing environmental political economy of the media is outlined by Mosco (2009). Environmentalism confronts both neoclassical and Marxian traditions as being dedicated to industrial growth, unimpeded technological development and the expansion of the means of production and materialist dominance over nature, while ignoring the economic value of nature and the consequences of treating the natural world and non-renewable resources as capital. Mosco argues that critical political economy's interest in environmentalism is in keeping with the field's social totality approach (incorporating the entire organic world) and its moral philosophy (extending moral vision beyond human life to all life processes) (2009, p. 61). In this vein, Maxwell and Miller (2012) draw attention to the growth of digital and Internet media technologies, addressing the perception that they are clean technologies against growing evidence of their toxicity, the poisonous working conditions facing manufacturing labour and the hazards these technologies produce as waste in their post-consumer life.

In a succession of books, Mark Andrejevic (2004, 2007, 2013) has placed a sophisticated critical political economy at the heart of understanding the highly interactive, digital media era. Instead of succumbing to the 'digital sublime' – Mosco's (2005) term for the exaggerated optimism about the democratisation, access and empowerment which interactive digital media may bring – Andrejevic analyses the heightened forms of surveillance and monitoring facilitated by the development of new media technologies. Hopeful amateurs willingly submit to minute-by-minute monitoring on reality TV (*Reality TV: The Work of Being Watched*). Intense interactions on social media platforms turn us all into 'lab rats' (*iSpy: Surveillance and Power in the Interactive Era*). Data miners, sentiment analysts and decision markets offer to steer us through the 'infoglut', but take away our human agency and beggar the public sphere (*Infoglut: How Too Much Information Is Changing the Way We Think and Know*).

Dal Yong Jin's (2010) detailed account of Korea's online gaming 'empire', for example, draws attention to the need to extend the field with depth and rigour beyond its largely Western focus. This is imperative because countries such as Korea 'lead the world in the development of online games' (Jin, 2010, p. 3). Jin's method of understanding how and why Korea attained such world leadership is exemplary – and anticipates key points we wish to make later in the chapter in assessing critical political economy. While securely based in political economy, Jin incorporates detailed attention to the roots of the national online game culture, distinct Korean modes of organisation of game playing (such as eSports, games played as sports by well-organised teams) and nationally specific aspects of new media labour and online game fandom.

The canonical emphasis on the large media corporation is taken to newly rigorous heights by Scott Fitzgerald (2012). Not only does he provide a penetrating framework that 'addresses broadly how privatisation, liberalisation, commercialisation and internationalisation have changed the media environment' (p. 16), Fitzgerald traces in detail the history of three of the world's major media corporations, Time Warner, Bertelsmann AG and News Corporation, showing how these forces in contemporary capitalism have driven expansion but threatened stability at the top of the media conglomerate pyramid.

Assessing political economy

Winseck's typology of political economy, including not only 'radical' or 'critical' political economy but also neoclassical economics, Schumpeterian institutional political economy and the cultural industries school, is very inclusive. However, it is highly unlikely that contemporary adherents to any of these latter schools would accept this classification. Attempts like those we have seen of Mosco to pose a set of shared goals (understanding historical change, totalistic view of social relations, moral philosophy and social praxis) suffer from an excessive level of generality. For example, the revolutionary social praxis, and its underpinning moral philosophy, of neo-Marxism is not the same as social democratic or liberal reformism. For this book, we treat neoclassical economics and critical political economy as distinct and quite fundamentally opposed frameworks, and regard institutional and evolutionary or Schumpeterian economics as significantly neglected within media, communication and cultural studies and therefore to be worthy of fresh reconsideration.

We also stress that the political economy framework has been the subject of extensive review and critique from *within* media, communication and cultural, over some decades, with crude base-superstructure models giving way to much more nuanced accounts of human agency, textual and audience/user productivity, and the institutional study of production, distribution and exhibition. Our comments here focus on those critiques that come from the media and cultural fields.

Winseck has argued that, in its focus upon the dominant power of monopoly capital, there is a tendency to view the media industries 'as a giant pyramid, with power concentrated at the top, and not enough attention paid to the details of key players, markets, and the dynamics and diversity that exist among all the elements that make up the media' (Winseck, 2011, p. 23). He argues that there is a pervasive tendency to overstate the extent to which market concentration has eliminated competition in and differences between media industries and to understate the diversity and complexity of the industries and the pervasive role of uncertainty across all levels of the media.

The foundational debates conducted between cultural studies and political economy in the 1970s and 1980s argued that political economy neglected the role of agency while stressing structural determinants in the time-honoured structure–agency dialectic in the social sciences. Stuart Hall was the main theorist who developed a politics of critical reading practice applied to popular media texts. Hall made considerable use of the work of Gramsci and the concepts of ideology and hegemony (Hall, 1986), and played a significant part in developing a form of post-Marxism concerned with discourse, representation and the new configurations of capitalism, identity and politics associated with the 'New Times' of post-1960s Western capitalism (Hall and Jacques, 1989). Following De Certeau and Foucault, Hall conceptualised the resistive practices of everyday life as always located within the space of power. His approach to analysis focuses on the scope for negotiation and opposition on the part of the audience, and, as there are no 'margins' outside of power from which to claim authenticity, political 'resistance' in contemporary culture occurs within and through consumption practices and not just in the spheres of industrial production, as audiences transform commodities and use the media. The politics of radical readership became a core concept of contemporary cultural studies. This was played out at the level of audience analysis, with arguments for the agency of the audience (e.g. John Fiske), in fashioning fan cultures (e.g. Henry Jenkins), reading against the grain (e.g. Leibes and Katz), and adaptations of uses and gratifications studies reasserting importance of neglected audiences and despised genres (e.g. Tania Modleski, Ien Ang).

Drawing on the British cultural studies tradition associated with Hall, John Fiske (1989) argued that audiences should not be seen as passive receptors of textual meaning that simply absorbed without modification meanings and messages from popular media, but rather as active readers able to produce meanings and value not tied to interpreting authorial intention. The meanings audiences produce are framed not only by the way the text is structured but by the social and cultural situations of audiences. The construction of meaning and the location of texts in daily life alter from culture to culture, and in terms of gender, class, race, ethnicity, sexuality and age within diverse cultural communities. While Fiske acknowledged that popular cultural texts are the products of capitalist corporations, his concern was with audience agency and with the counter-power of audiences as resistant readers.

Henry Jenkins (1992) took the agency of the audience further, speaking of 'textual poachers' to describe those audiences who 'appropriate popular texts and re-read them in a fashion that serves different interests, as spectators who transform the watching of TV into a rich and complex participatory culture' (1992, p. 346). Jenkins describes fan cultures as participatory cultures, bounded by *affiliations* (formal and informal membership to online fan communities), *expressions* (creating new cultural forms such as sampling, fan fiction, mash-ups, cosplay, zines), *collaborative problem-solving* (working together to develop new knowledge forms such as Wikis) and *circulations* (shaping the flow of media through podcasting and blogging). Jenkins would later extend studies of critical fandom to new media and convergent media, arguing that 'top-down' corporate industrial and promotional strategies were only successful insofar as they were developed in collaboration with the bottom-up practices of fans of the programmes and content in question.

Elihu Katz and Tamar Liebes (1984, 1990) contested the idea that textual meanings were fixed, rejecting the assertion that the widespread global appeal of American television content was part of a process of cultural imperialism, providing copious and intriguing evidence that audiences can and do 'read against the grain'. Cultural imperialism, they argued, presumes that there is an inherently American message in a given text and that this message is not only perceived by audiences but it is 'perceived in the same way by viewers in different cultures' (Katz and Liebes, 1984, p. 28). Tracking the reception of CBS's long-running prime time soap opera *Dallas*, Katz and Liebes argued that viewers used such programmes as a forum to reflect on their own identities, becoming involved morally (comparing the programmes characters with themselves and their socio-familial lives), playfully ('trying on' unfamiliar roles), ideologically (searching for manipulative messages) and aesthetically (discerning the formulae from which the programme is constructed). Ien Ang (1985) also reconstructed the pleasures of watching *Dallas* offered for Dutch viewers, concluding that *Dallas* viewers were actively involved in the production of a range of responses that are not reducible to the surface meanings of the text. Ang's work helped to establish a new forum for feminist interest in popular culture, women's genres and women readers.

The active audience strand of cultural studies research was widely critiqued by political economists for its perceived 'cultural populism' (McGuigan, 1992), and apparent disinterest in the corporate and industrial structures of capitalist media (Golding and Ferguson, 1997). Curran (1990) argued that what he termed the 'new revisionism' in audience research had parallels in the earlier debates in mass communication theory between those who argued strong and negative media effects, and alternative approaches such as the 'uses and gratifications' tradition, which had identified the pleasures of meaning that audiences could derive from media texts, and the social determinants of different readings of media content. A sometimes acrimonious 'political economy versus cultural studies' debate took place. Nicholas Garnham (1995) argued the primacy of the economic, as it provided the material framework (capitalism as a mode of production) through which cultural and symbolic practices occurred. Against this, Lawrence Grossberg (1995) argued that such approaches were reductionist in making cultural practice the by-product of economic determinants and that cultural studies theorists 'believe that culture matters and that it cannot be treated (dismissed) as the transparent ... public face of dominative and manipulative capitalists' (Grossberg, 1995, p. 76).

The passion once associated with this debate has died down somewhat, partly due to the interest of cultural studies theorists in researching questions of production, work and industry as well as consumption, culture and identity, as seen in recent work from a cultural economy perspective (e.g. Sinclair, 2011). This did, however, leave open the question of what theory of audiences political economists chose to work with, and whether it did in fact largely read audience practices off industrial structures, seeing the consumers of popular culture as subordinated to a dominant ideology as expressed in media texts. It was this approach derived from orthodox Marxism, with its 'residual and merely reflective role assigned to "the cultural"' (Hall, 1986, p. 39), that cultural studies had been particularly concerned to contest.

Internal debates within the discipline that sought to nuance the top-down approach of political economy and better understand the interplay between human agency and economic structure also focused on the conditions under which media were actually produced, with a focus on production cultures, production houses and what Thomas Schatz (2010 [1989]) called the 'genius in the system', or anthropologist Hortense Powdermaker (1950) called the 'dream factory'. This approach has typically focused on accounting for the complexities of large-scale industrial systems such as Hollywood (Bordwell *et al.*, 1985), public service broadcasting such as the BBC (Born, 2005) and the bounded creativity of producers, production houses or directors within those systems. While some of these studies are largely descriptive, a driving concern has been what innovative, qualitative difference could be achieved inside powerful, hegemonic systems of capitalist meaning-production. Schatz (2010 [1989]) suggested that greater attention and credit should be awarded to producers and executives who created studio styles in the period of classical Hollywood. Schatz studies classical Hollywood as a functioning *system*, 'a melding of institutional forces' (2010, p. 6) into an altogether complex configuration where writer, director, star, cinematographer, artistic director and costume designer 'work' in fusion with production operations, marketing and sales strategies, corporate structures and managerial systems. Bordwell *et al.* (1985) go further in their monumental study of the classical Hollywood system, showing how the storytelling demands of the system often trumped economic considerations.

These negotiated responses to critical political economy have been heartland concerns for cultural and media studies on and off for decades, and will continue. At present, there is the burgeoning subfield of production cultures studies, and grounded, anthropologically informed approaches to culturally diverse audiences. Caldwell (2008) argues that for scholars to fully understand the production of culture and cultural artefacts, they must explore the culture of production. In his ethnographic study of the labour practices of Hollywood's behind-the-scenes workers, Caldwell treats the film and television production communities as 'themselves cultural expressions and entities involving all of the symbolic processes and collective practices that other cultures use' (2008, p. 2). He examines how workers critically reflect upon their labour, asserting that this self-awareness and self-analysis directly informs production practices, media text and audience reception and shows how this self-reflexivity shifts based on employment status within the industry. Rather than focusing on the well-researched and easily recognised role of the television producer – those working in roles requiring creative conceptualisation, managerial or financial control – Mayer (2011) focuses on below-the-line labour (such as television set assemblers, soft-core camera operators, reality television casters and volunteer cable advocates) and their agency in the systems of television production.

Power – The central question for political economy

A curious feature of these heartland debates in media, communications and cultural studies is that they have done little to conceptually advance our understanding of the foundations on which a contemporary media economics could proceed. In the absence of extended debate about the types of economics appropriate to the contemporary media, a fairly stale recycling of the neoclassical-critical political economy debate stands in for intellectual advancement in the field. Meanwhile, for many at the cutting edges of our field, these debates are virtually over, with actor-network theory (ANT) and its variants now throwing a sociological envelope over what constitutes the society–culture–economy triad. As seen, for example, in the *Journal of Cultural Economy*, there is a pursuit of a micro-empiricism where conceptual claims can only be made from close observation of particular objects themselves.

This book is focused on the need in our disciplines to get a handle on strands in heterodox economics that are alternatives to political economy and ANT-inspired cultural economy, which have been more effective within the economics discipline in critiquing and modifying the dominant neoclassical paradigm than political economy. But before we discuss institutional economics and evolutionary economics, we need to focus on the question that is at the core of the political economy approach – the question of power.

The question of power is at the base of critical political economy of the media. The notion of power is fundamental to much political theory and philosophy and also underpins the very notion of the term 'political economy' – the idea that the economy, rather than existing as an autonomous domain, is inextricably tied to political process, intent and actors. But 'power' is such an all-encompassing term that we need to break it down into its constituent parts. John Thompson (1995, pp. 16–17) has identified four forms of power:

1. Political – institutions and practices primarily concerned with coordination and regulation; this form of power is primarily held through government and the state;
2. Economic – the ability to control processes of production, distribution, prices in markets and accumulation; such power is most notably held by corporations, but may also be held by other institutional agents, such as trade unions or producers' associations;
3. Coercive – the capacity to use actual or potential force against others, particularly in combination with political power, notably associated with the armed forces, the police, security agencies and so on;
4. Cultural/symbolic – power associated with the ability to control the production, transmission and reception of symbolic forms, or the means of information and communication.

The fundamental assumption of political economy is that large-scale economic actors in the media field – the Hollywood Majors, the large telecommunications companies, television networks, cable companies, the emerging leviathans of search and online services – exercise great power (perhaps supervening power) over what is produced, how it is produced and possibly also, in some of the cruder versions, how it is received. This is *economic* power – 'the ability to control processes of production, distribution, prices in markets, and accumulation' – and there is little, apart from the major contests over agency at the point of reception, that is questionable here.

At its core, political economy assumes that power emanates from the ability to control the means of production and accumulation and flows from the top echelons of society to the bottom. It also posits stronger versions of the alignment of, or homology between, economic, political and cultural/symbolic power, assuming that economic power results in the ability to exercise political and cultural/symbolic power. But the ways in which powerful economic actors may also exercise political and/or cultural/symbolic power cannot be decided in advance, as there is no universal template or prescription for how such alignment can be achieved. Further, the concept of power, as deployed in critical political economy of the media, is what Michel Foucault (1991) would call 'domination'. Foucault defines power more generally, with domination as a subset. When it comes to industries which inherently combine economic power with political and cultural/symbolic influence like the media, we tend to side with Foucault's understanding that power is inherently relational, contingent, unstable and reversible, and resistance is a necessary and inevitable corollary of such power.

In what follows, we put both of these caveats on the question of power to work.

Economic and political power

The strongest version of economic power mapped to political power is the propaganda model developed by Chomsky and Herman. In this model, the media are presented as the instruments of the dominant classes, who are 'able to filter the news...marginalise dissent, and allow...dominant interests to get their messages across to the public' (Herman and Chomsky, 1988, p. 2). Very few critical political economists would agree with this extreme functionalism. A more mainstream position is that adopted by Golding and Murdock, who argue that economic power dominates, but that 'owners, advertisers and key political personnel cannot always do as they wish... [but] operate within structures that constrain as well as facilitate' (2005, p. 63). And Graeme Murdock (1982) has emphasised the clear distinction between allocative and operational control: the former belongs to governing boards and shareholding structures and the latter to senior management. The ability to convert economic to political influence is strongest where there is strong alignment across these levels.

Clearly, with very large companies, particularly if they are multinationals, operate in oligopolistic markets and work in information as well as entertainment, the probability they may be able to exercise significant political muscle is high. This also depends on the strategic intent of those who are in a position to direct the company towards such ends. The outstanding example is Rupert Murdoch.

Economic and political power: Rupert Murdoch

Murdoch has thrived for nearly 60 years in the media business and still wields significant political power. He has decisively shaped United States, British and Australian politics over the past 30 years – beginning with the election of the Reagan and Thatcher governments in the 1980s – in an effort to entrench his own global corporate interests in Australia, the United Kingdom and the United States.

Interest in Murdoch has generated a very significant and constantly growing body of literature that is remarkably consistent in its findings (Munster, 1985; Neil, 1996; Chenoweth, 2001; Page, 2003; Shawcross, 2003; Dover, 2007; Wolff, 2008; Fitzgerald 2012; McKnight, 2012; Watson and Hickman, 2012). Suggesting that Murdoch's ideas are 'among the most influential in the world and have formed part of the conservative revolution in thinking over the last 30 years' and that they are 'shared by many powerful people and have already transformed the economic and social institutions of many nations' (McKnight, 2012, p. 12), David McKnight argues that Murdoch sees himself as an outsider fighting society elites despite his own privileged background and multimillionaire status; that he claims to be anti-elitist, posing as the champion of the 'everyday' person; that he finances, popularises and proselytises politics based on privatisation, competition, free markets and deregulation; and that he promotes populist conservatism through opinionated and sensational news reporting. Page (2003) argues that investigations of political activity and state institutions are calibrated to target unfavoured and enhance favoured politicians and parties and that News Corp synergistically uses its media outlets to support its own commercial interests. McKnight (2012) also chronicles the creation and rise of Fox News, noting how Murdoch and the network's chief, Roger Ailes, subverted from within the commitment of mainstream news media to balance in reporting. McKnight gives particular regard to the coverage of climate change across News Corp outlets: 'In this "balanced" framework, scientific findings would appear controversial, since the premise of the debate was politics: the sub-text was that support or opposition to climate science was a matter of political belief. [...] Murdoch and Ailes created a politicised business model that ultimately contributed both profits and political influence to News Corporation' (McKnight, 2012, pp. 162–63). But, ultimately, corporate interests win over political agendas: following the News of the World phone

(Continued)

hacking scandal, Watson and Hickman (2012) document how News Corporation has misused its media power for corporate gain, at times resorting to illegal means to obtain stories that often have little, if any, public importance and thus the ability to directly impact the political process.

Set against these sorry tales of the suborning of the public sphere by economic power wielded for political ends is the need to take seriously the classic liberal democratic claim for the role of the state to give voice and agency through representation to the less powerful, mitigating economic power. Critical political economy tends to play down struggles *between* economic and political power, especially where the latter has successfully sequestered – usually through regulation – untoward economic power. Institutional economics can give us a more balanced perspective and is the subject of Chapter 3, while the very significant role of the state in establishing media institutions, such as PSBs, is discussed in Chapter 5.

Economic and cultural/symbolic power

The assumption that economic power produces cultural/symbolic power is both highly seductive and dramatic as well as most difficult to properly evidence. Early versions of critical political economy were much more ready to make totalising claims about this link. But, as we have seen in the earlier part of this chapter, a couple of decades of cultural studies' reworkings of notions of cultural power have seen successive recalibrations in the claims of critical political economy.

Stuart Ewan's *Captains of Consciousness* (1976) suggested that American industrial capitalists were, through advertising, trying to control the entire social realm. He argued that advertising was an attempt to deflect dissatisfied consumers attentions away from the consumer products themselves, and from the systems that produced them, towards their own internal desires; encouraging them to substitute social and political desires for ever-larger purchases of consumer commodities in a quest for self-improvement. Ewan argues that over time advertising has led American consumers away from family and community as the source of common value (in regards of labour, family life, sexual relations, etc.) and into the grasp of the corporate 'captains of consciousness'.

Economic and cultural/symbolic power: The Disney corporation

Janet Wasko (2001) undertakes a major study of the Disney corporation. She traces its progression from a modest animation studio to a multinational mass media corporation – one that now has over 166,000 employees and boasts revenues of US$42.28 billion (The Walt Disney Company, 2012). Wasko argues that despite the familiar capitalist corporate practices that fuelled Disney growth (strict management and labour practices, the adoption of new technologies and techniques, merchandising and cross-promotional initiatives, control and enforcement of copyright and intellectual property, multifaceted entertainment and leisure diversification), Disney has consistently maintained a 'magical' aura through its use of 'Classic Disney' themes and values that include individualism, escapism, innocence and romance across the bulk of its textual products (film and television, entertainment, theme parks, etc.).

While Wasko limits her claims, others go much further. Giroux and Pollock (2010), for example, disparage Disney for whitewashing history and presenting the past in a nostalgic light, for promoting sexism and racism and for encouraging massive consumer spending while assuming the guise of innocuous family fun. They argue that The Walt Disney Company has undue influence over the developing minds of children as its 'magical' aura masks its promotion of consumerism over education and creative play. Bryman (2001) has suggested that the principles of Disney that are particular to its theme parks have come to dominate society, particularly in terms of theming, dedifferentiation of consumption, merchandising and emotional labour.

Other Disney scholars challenge these claims of panoptic power. Choi (2012) takes the case of Hong Kong Disneyland (HKDL). Choi writes that HKDL was promoted as the 'Millennium Dream Comes True!' in 1999, but viewed as 'Hong Kong's shame' after its opening in 2005, arguing that while Disney brought Hong Kong a physical park, non-transparent values and related management practices, visitors consume the park in a local way that Disneyland management finds difficult to control, while local labour produce and circulate new meanings of 'Disney' and change certain Disney policies.

Economic power

Let us look a little more closely at the question of economic power. Critical political economy of the media tends to analyse big business. Some of the classic studies are those of world-spanning conglomerates, such as News Corporation, Bertelsmann, Time Warner and Disney (Bagdikian, 1983, 2004; Murdock, 1990; Barnouw and Gitlin, 1998; McChesney, 1999; Wasko, 2001; Fitzgerald, 2012). Indeed, some of the biggest companies in the world have been, or are, media, information and communication concerns or those that have these concerns as part of their conglomerate structures. Almost by definition, the operations of these businesses exercise great economic influence and, it is assumed, in concert they exercise even greater power. What these studies tend not to do is focus on the struggles *within* economic elites; typically intense struggles which produce the kinds of 'creative destruction' *within* capitalism which Joseph Schumpeter (1934, 1942) regarded as its fundamental characteristic. 'Creative destruction' is a way of understanding the ceaseless volatility of capitalism and the opportunities for entrepreneurial agency it opens even as it destroys old orders. We explore the concept in Chapter 4.

While there has been remarkable stability at the top echelons in the screen business, for example, there is evidence that firms which have long dominated the mass media may now face the most serious challenge in their history – as we explore in Chapter 5. This focus on power struggles *within* economic elites contrasts with the assumption that elites reinforce each other's power and influence and present as a more-or-less unified bloc against democracy, nation states and citizens. The former perspective draws on strands of elite theory more so than on neo-Marxist theories for theoretical support. Elite theory affirms that power is centred on elites, but that power centres are not guaranteed and can change over time. Elite theory has its origins in the political sociology of Gaetano Mosca, Vilfredo Pareto, Robert Michels and Max Weber (Higley, 2010). It is a highly critical account of the endemic and possibly ineradicably unequal distribution of power between minority elites and population majorities. This can be linked to Schumpeterian accounts of the ceaseless volatility of the distribution of power blocs within capitalism to shape a non-teleological, non-totalistic but nonetheless critical account of battles within capitalist elites and the outcomes these battles may have for consumer and citizen populations. This perspective also correlates with Lash and Urry's (1987) notion of 'disorganised capitalism'.

Critical political economy's focus on big business skews the question of power radically towards a top-down focus – what Foucault would call domination rather than power. But the vast majority of media firms and agents in market economies are not big businesses, and the small business and its fortunes is the reality for the large proportion of media workers. A political economy of these small-, medium- and micro-sized enterprises would focus on their economic subaltern status, as they attempt the judo move of using the power of their opponents or competitors against them, or just to stay in the game. As Foucault says, resistance is a necessary corollary of power.

The structure of media industries often is characterised by a small number of large aggregators (ISPs, search), distributors (movies), broadcasters or publishers (games, print) and a large number of small content suppliers, quite often dispersed widely, even globally. This is the phenomenon of the 'missing middle', a middle layer of medium-sized firms often characteristic of more conventional industries (see Flew, 2012, p. 184). This power asymmetry is, rightly, focused on by critical political economy.

Economic power: The games industry

In the games industry, for example, where this power asymmetry is clear, the focus should be, according to Toby Miller, on 'domination by firms that buy up or destroy small businesses and centralise power in the metropole; decimation of little bedroom concerns in favour of giant conglomerates' (Miller, 2008, p. 232).

Certainly, there are a few very large, very powerful publishers in the global games industry (Electronic Arts, Sony, Nintendo), although equal stress could be placed on the huge creative disruption wrought on the incumbents by mobile gaming established on the new digital platforms run by contending economic elites (Apple, Facebook, Android platforms). The emphasis from critical political economy that centres on globally dominant firms, their hegemonic control and the labour conditions they auspice might also be balanced by a focus on the issues faced by local production industries in the context of this global industry and questions of business strategy as the viability of the SME firm's articulation into the global system becomes paramount. A regular feature, as Miller acerbically observes, of the global games system are buyouts of small firms which show promise

(Continued)

by dominant publishers. These carry obvious dangers such as asset stripping and loss of local intellectual property. But the reality is more complex, as such buyouts may also be the difference between survival and liquidation for companies which are vulnerable to the 'creative destruction' wrought in an industry with such rapid innovation cycles. There are more and more instances of reasonably sustainable independent games development alongside of and separate from the axis of developers making games for the conglomerate publishers. In Australia, for example, there is the success of indie developer HalfBrick releasing games such as *Fruit Ninja*. And Korean games culture, canvassed earlier in the chapter, sees robust synergies between production and consumption at the national level. The games industry is high risk and the likelihood of economic and commercial success is quite small (Sandqvist, 2012, p. 149). Nevertheless, there has been very rapid growth in small business content creators around mobile gaming, and these should receive as much attention as the hegemons do.

Another example can be drawn from studies of 'Global' Hollywood which focus on the world-spanning activities of US-dominated film and high-end television production as a classic instance of footloose capital seeking the most economically advantageous locales for production, undermining United States-based unions and suborning the cultural diversity of their sometime hosts in numerous outposts around the world (Miller *et al.*, 2005). But, as Goldsmith, Ward and O'Regan (2010; see also Gasher, 2002; Tinic, 2005) emphasise, you can also focus on the judo move of negotiating with and resistance to power involved in what they call 'Local Hollywoods', rather than an exclusive focus on domination. They argue,

Global Hollywood captures only one side of the story. We need to restore to view the myriad complementary and initiatory actions of smaller players and places.... The top-down perspective needs to be balanced by an examination of the critical role played by the many location interests, the many Local Hollywoods...it is only through fine-grained, place-focused analysis that the terms and circumstances of a place's engagement with Hollywood can be understood. This means acknowledging a subtle negotiation of control.

(Goldsmith, Ward and O'Regan, 2010, pp. 28–29)

A close examination of media industry developers, policy activists and reformers around the globe would show that the great majority of them are focused on precisely this kind of judo move. Informed and influenced by critical political economy's typical focus on domination by large multinational corporations and their capacity to influence the political and cultural/symbolic realms, they nevertheless must work to create sustainable small and medium enterprises, and champion cultural specificity and supportive state policies.

Conclusion: The debate continues...

As a lively testament to its currency, contemporary defences and critical reassessments of critical political economy abound. In concluding this chapter, we pay particular attention to Eileen Meehan and Janet Wasko's (2013) passionate defence of its salience against its critics, on the one hand, and Nicholas Garnham's (Garnham, 2011; Garnham and Fuchs, 2014) forensic critique of some of its contemporary tendencies, on the other.

Meehan and Wasko's article looks to set the record straight about 'radical' political economy in the light of its 'misrepresentation' and 'caricature' by those advancing sub-disciplinary *foci* such as media industries studies, media economics, screen industry studies, production studies or creative industries studies. They set the scene by focusing on the 'politics of nomenclature' in the United States. The embrace of the term 'critical' (as code for, while avoiding, the term 'Marxist' or neo-Marxist) is because of a history of state persecution of leftists generally, and Marxists specifically, for over a century. This is very important and reminds us of the important differences in academic culture between the main zones of academic work in the field – the United States and United Kingdom/Europe. It underlines that critical political economy has won a place in the American academy through hard-fought struggle and against powerful, dominant ideologies and an ensconced system of mainstream 'administrative' media and communication studies. It has taken a significant degree of courage for many to work in critical political economy in the United States.

Thus, Meehan and Wasko are concerned to maintain hard boundaries around what constitutes US critical political economy, limning its proud history over some decades. They make a powerful case that it has proved extremely flexible in dealing – against many of its critics – with entertainment as well as information media, with human agency and initiative as much as structure and control, and by demonstrating that it is more than capable of embracing and incorporating the challenges of cultural studies, media ethnography and audience research. But one might doubt whether all the examples offered of methodological eclecticism and synthesis leave critical political economy completely untouched in terms of some of its core assumptions. These remain firmly neo-Marxist, requiring 'ruthless criticism' of a capitalist order that, though riven with contradiction, remains sufficiently total in its effect on all aspects of life that it requires a singular, or total, framework to explain and respond to it. There can be no truck with the celebratory, reformist, middle-range approaches that render the study of media production in a 'palatable form for cultural analysts, policy wonks, and the media industry itself' (Meehan and Wasko, 2013, p. 49).

This is clear from their strident dismissal of Jennifer Holt and Alisa Perren's (2009) outline of their approach to the field in *Media Industries: History, Theory, and Method* and Timothy Havens, Amanda Lotz and Serra Tinic's (2009) 'Critical Media Industry Studies: A Research Approach'. Let us consider just the first of these.

Holt and Perren's approach in *Media Industries: History, Theory, and Method* is first to take fully on board what the object of study actually is – everything, as they say, 'from "mobisodes" design for iPhones and the labour force manufacturing plasma television sets in Malaysia to the Creative Commons movement and trade shows in Budapest', and the fact that such an 'object' has been studied in 'film and television studies, communication, law, public policy, business, economics, journalism, and sociology departments' (2009, p. 1). Then, a comprehensive account of the dynamics and forces of change in the media industries is necessary, and such an account will equally be tendered by a range of disciplinary perspectives. In the face of this, the usual response is to adopt a weak pluralistic position – any approach is as valid as another. Rather, Holt and Perren adopt what we would call strong pluralism and a progressive reformist cultural politics. Without attempting to paper over methodological difference, they suggest that media industries scholarship of whatever methodological or ideological stripe should strive to *integrate* analyses of media texts, audiences, histories and culture. This would 'enable more productive scholarship' (2009, p. 2). So the selection criteria for the essays in their field-defining text is that they

> attend to constructs of text and image as they relate to industrial structure and economics, connect politics and policy to issues of art and audience, and develop theoretical and methodological paradigms that not only engage with the past but also offer ways of thinking about media industries in the present (and presumably future) landscape of convergence.
>
> (2009, p. 4)

The object of study is constitutively plural in its nature and cannot be grasped through a single analytical optic. This looks, to us, not a long way from some of the integrative studies extolled by Meehan and Wasko. And certainly it is exemplified in works we have mentioned, such as Jin's study of the Korean games industry and culture.

This is a good segue to a contemporary European/UK hotspot of debate around critical political economy. At the University of Westminster, Christian Fuchs is leading a reassertion of Marxist-inspired political economy and recently engaged in an extended dialogue, 'Revisiting the Political Economy of Communication', with one of the leading pioneers of the political economy of media, culture and communications, Nicholas Garnham, also of the University of Westminster (Garnham and Fuchs, 2014).

As one of the pioneers of the political economy approach to culture and communications, Nicholas Garnham's critiques are even more far-reaching. His argument is that 'the term "political economy" ... has become a euphemism for a vague, crude and un-self-questioning form of Marxism, linked to a gestural and self-satisfied, if often paranoid, radicalism', which he considers to be 'both empirically questionable and theoretically and politically dubious' (Garnham, 2011, p. 42). Garnham has argued that 'a crude and unexamined romantic Marxist rejection of the market per se ... has blocked analysis of how actual markets work and with what effects', meaning that 'it has not taken the economics in PE [political economy] with the seriousness it deserves and requires' (Garnham, 2011, p. 42).

In contrast to a strong but overly simple narrative which says that power is becoming more concentrated in fewer hands, Garnham asks whether the media and cultural policy environment is in fact far more complex than simple market/state dichotomies would suggest. In particular, he questions whether one can make any general claims about the ideological content of commercial media. Returning – somewhat ironically – to propositions first raised in cultural studies, Garnham argues that the rise of capitalist modernity sees societies becoming more internally complex and heterogeneous, with one consequence of growing social complexity being that cultural producers seeking to make a profit have an increasingly strong economic interest in producing for more diverse cultural markets, producing for multiple niches rather than for homogeneous mass markets. For Garnham, cultural production under capitalism is not characterised by ideologically driven censorship or insufficient diversity of content. Instead, he has proposed that capitalism has made more cultural product available and 'has clearly widened cultural diversity on both a national and international scale, even if it continues to be unevenly spread' (Garnham, 2011, p. 45). As capitalist modernity is characteristically associated with the declining salience of rule on the basis of power over the distribution of ideas – what Max Weber termed the 'disenchantment of the world' – Garnham considers it ironic that many political economists remain attached to the dominant ideology thesis given that 'a capitalist economic system was compatible with a wide range of political and social systems' and that 'the industrialisation of cultural production and distribution had produced just that breakdown of ideological control that the original feudal and religious opponents of modernity and capitalism feared' (Garnham, 2011, p. 45).

In his extended dialogue with Christian Fuchs, Garnham comes to conclusions not dissimilar to those of Holt and Perren:

My main argument with many of the versions of the return to Marxism today [is] they share exactly the same worldview as the so-called neoliberals. They think there is one solution to the problem. One thinks that the market will solve everything, the other that doing away with the market will.

(Garnham and Fuchs, 2014, p. 121)

Critical political economy of the media remains, as it should, a central perspective in the field of media studies. The heritage of political economy is broad and very deep – as Meehan and Wasko remind us (2013, p. 40), Adam Smith, Karl Marx, Joseph Schumpeter, Alfred Marshall and John Maynard Keynes were all political economists of their day. That is the quite defensible basis on which Winseck can be so catholic in his claims for political economy. But we think it is doubtful today that it makes contemporary analytical sense to claim critical political economy as the progenitor of any worthwhile approach to the economic and industrial structure of media that does not adhere to neoclassical principles. And while we have noted, with Meehan and Wasko, on the one hand, and Holt and Perren, on the other, the growing calls for and (with Jin on the Korean games industry) the practice of inclusive and diverse approaches to media, we have also seen that the theoretical and ideological debate remains very lively. We have touched on contemporary alternatives *within* the discipline field – media industries studies, media economics, production studies and creative industries. Now, we want to turn to two broad fields within economics itself which, we hope, may introduce useful new perspectives, approaches and emphases into media studies.

3 Institutional Economics

Institutional approaches have a long history in the social sciences, although their status in the history of economic thought is a contested one. In fields such as political science, it has been argued by authors such as Guy Peters (2012, p. 3) that the field was institutional from the beginning, as it has always been interested in the ways in which different societies have responded to the challenge of how 'the mercurial and fickle nature of individual behaviour, and the need to direct that behaviour towards collective purposes, required formal political institutions'. In other disciplines, the influence of institutional approaches has shifted over time. In sociology, an interest in institutions was a significant feature of the work of Max Weber, Karl Polanyi and Emile Durkheim, and institutions feature strongly in the *new economic sociology* and its understanding of markets, organisations and networks. Others have argued that the focus in neo-Marxist theories upon macro-social structures can mitigate against the study of specific institutions, and how the conduct of social agents within such environments serve to shape the social field (e.g. Hindess, 1989; Hays, 1994). By contrast, institutional approaches are very much associated with *middle range theorising*, of the sort pioneered in sociology by Robert Merton (Merton, 1968; c.f. Turner, 2009) and developed in contemporary social sciences by authors such as Anthony Giddens with his concept of *structuration* (Giddens, 1984), which sought to overcome the dichotomy between social structures and individual agency.

It has been harder to establish a tradition of institutional analysis in economics. As discussed in Chapter 1, neoclassical economics has drawn upon methodological individualism and rational choice theory as the foundations for understanding economic behaviour. From these individualistic starting points, it is thus assumed that 'all statements about the properties of "collectivities" – groups, institutions, societies – can be reduced to statements about the properties of individuals' (Ingham, 1996, pp. 245–46). Neoclassical theory has characteristically explained the existence of institutions as arising from choices made by individuals to act collectively, based on rational criteria for maximising personal wellbeing. Critics of neoclassical economics have long argued that this strong individualism, where 'the self-governing individual constitutes the ultimate unit of the social sciences, and that all social phenomena resolve themselves into decisions and actions of individuals' (Hodgson, 2007, p. 213), loses sight of the formative influence of history and culture, as given concrete form through institutions, upon the behaviours and preferences of individuals.

The critique of methodological individualism, and its associated neglect of how culture and institutions shape human behaviour, has long been a key feature of what is known as the *old institutional economics*, which has been in existence since Thorstein Veblen's work in the late 19th century. The institutionalist tradition in economics was carried forward in the North American context by authors such as Clarence Ayres, J. R. Commons and Wesley Mitchell, and later by dissenters from neoclassical orthodoxy such as John Kenneth Galbraith. Among the features of such an institutional approach have been an empirical approach to understanding the economy, in contrast to what is seen as overly abstract theorising of the neoclassical school; an ongoing interest in the evolutionary development of capitalism, and the interaction between technology, institutions and culture; and an expectation that advances in economic thinking need to occur in dialogue with sociology, politics, history and the social sciences (Rutherford, 1994, pp. 9–20; Stilwell, 2002, pp. 209–18; Hodgson, 2004). An important bridge between the 'old' institutionalism and communications theory is found in the Canadian communications tradition, with Harold Innis' analysis of the ways in which media technologies structure relations of power and patterns of social interaction, including the social shaping of markets and economic institutions (Melody, 1987; Crowley and Heyer, 1991).

The *new institutional economics* has emerged in part out of a recognition that the bracketing off of economics from other academic disciplines and fields of research has come at some cost to economics. In his lecture delivered upon receiving the 1993 Nobel Prize in Economics, Douglass North observed that economics had cut itself off from history, neglecting the historically evolving role of institutions and the significance of how such institutions develop over time. This affected its ability not only to 'shed new light on the economic past' but also to 'provide an analytical framework that will enable us to understand economic change' (North, 1994, p. 359). The absence of a theory of economic dynamics is particularly deleterious, North argued, when it comes to considering questions of economic development and the forms of advice that economists should be giving policy-makers and politicians. North argued that:

> The very methods employed by neoclassical economics have dictated the subject matter and militated against such a development. That theory in the pristine form that gave it mathematical precision and elegance modelled a frictionless and static world... ignored the incentive structure embodied in institutions... [and] contained two erroneous assumptions: (i) that institutions do not matter and (ii) that time does not matter.
>
> (North, 1994, p. 359)

In this chapter, we consider institutional economics in its traditional forms, associated with economists such as Thorstein Veblen and John Kenneth Galbraith, and the emergence of the NIE, with particular reference to the work of Douglass North and Oliver Williamson. One important difference we identify between the 'old' and 'new' institutional economics is their relationship to mainstream neoclassical theory. Early institutionalists were strongly hostile to the theoretical abstractions of conventional economics, arguing that its leading theorists lost sight of the importance of culture, customs and history in their pursuit of modelling elegance and mathematical rigour. The NIE approach, by contrast, has stressed its continuities with mainstream microeconomics, particularly in retaining the architecture of rational choice theory in its analyses of individual behaviour and that of individuals within institutions. Indeed, in some instances it extends rational choice theory from economic institutions to political ones, as with the theory of rent-seeking, where it is argued that politicians use public funds for vote-maximising purposes, government agencies seek to maximise state funding and so on, in ways that are at odds with the presumption that government regulators primarily serve the public interest.

The chapter will also consider the pioneering contributions of Max Weber, Emile Durkheim and Karl Polanyi to the new economic sociology associated with understanding markets as institutions, organisational behaviour and network sociology. One reason for this is to draw out elements of complementarity in the study of institutions between economics and sociology. For example, questions of trust and reciprocity, the socially and culturally embedded nature of markets and economic institutions and the importance of historical evolution in understanding the deep structure of institutional arrangements are all important to NIE, but its ongoing affinities to neoclassical economics present difficulties in developing a comprehensive understanding of these forces. At the same time, there are important points of ongoing differentiation between institutional economics and economic sociology: the latter tends to be closer to critical political economy on policy issues, contrasting sharply with the sometimes radically deregulationist agenda of some NIE theorists. The case studies in this chapter apply institutional insights to topics in media economics such as the role played by contracts in media industries, the institutions of global media policy, and the nature of broadcasting property and the role played by licences in allocating ownership.

Institutions and institutionalisms

The economist Geoffrey Hodgson has defined institutions in the following way:

> Institutions are durable systems of established and embedded social rules and conventions that structure social interactions.... In part, the durability of institutions stems from the fact that they can usefully create stable expectations of the behaviour of others. Generally, institutions enable ordered thought, expectation and action, by imposing form and consistency on human activities. They depend on the thoughts and actions of individuals but are not reducible to them.
>
> (Hodgson, 2003, p. 163)

Several points can be drawn from this definition:

1. Institutions have a history that enables them to be durable over time;
2. Institutions include formal organisations such as firms, trade unions, government agencies, universities and so on, but also include rules, habits, customs and conventions, of both a formal and an informal nature;
3. Institutions shape the behaviour of individuals and how they interact with one another;
4. Institutions do not necessarily exist 'outside' of individuals, as they shape the thoughts, expectations and actions of individuals;
5. At the same time, institutions have a concrete form that is over and above simply being the consequence of the rational decisions of individuals.

There are generally considered to be three strands of institutionalist thought in the social sciences (Hall and Taylor, 1996; Peters, 2012). The first is *historical institutionalism*, as seen in the work of authors such as Evans *et al.* (1985), Skocpol (1992), Evans (1995) and Hall and Soskice (2001). These theorists place a strong emphasis upon the *path dependency* of institutions and how they evolve over time, and the various ways in which 'the range of possibilities for that development will have been constrained by the formative period of that institution' (Peters, 2012, p. 73).

The second is *rational choice institutionalism*, sometimes used synonymously with the new institutional economics. Douglass North, one of the leaders of the new institutional economics, proposed that 'institutions form the incentive structure of a society, and the political and economic institutions, in consequence, are the underlying determinants of economic performance' (North, 1994, p. 359). Of particular importance in the rational choice approach is *strategic calculation*, and the ways in which 'an actor's behaviour is likely to be driven...by the actor's expectations about how others are likely to behave as well' (Hall and Taylor, 1996, p. 945). If the 'rules of the game' in particular societies suggest that there are significant gains to be made from cooperation, for instance, this will act to encourage the formation of collective institutions. In terms of the analysis of 'exit' and 'voice' pioneered by Alfred Hirschmann (1970), there will be formation of institutions that maximise collective voice, particularly in the political sphere. In the field of broadcast media, for example, the important role played by government in the allocation of operating licences has encouraged private broadcasters to form strong lobby groups to promote their interests with legislators and to deal with regulators in an ongoing manner.

Finally, *sociological institutionalism* refers both to the study of institutions found in the sociological 'classics', such as Max Weber, Emile Durkheim and Karl Polanyi, and to contemporary analyses of institutions as core sites through which individuals are culturally and cognitively shaped (Douglas, 1986; Zucker, 1987; Campbell, 1998). From this perspective, institutions are 'not only formal rules, procedures or norms, but also the symbol systems, cognitive scripts, and moral templates that provide the "frames of meaning" guiding human action' (Hall and Taylor, 1996, p. 947). An important implication of the sociological approach is that it blurs the lines between 'institutions' and 'culture', drawing attention both to the cultural dimensions of institutions and the importance of institutional cultures (March and Olsen, 1989; Clegg *et al.*, 2005) and to the manner in which markets themselves are cultural and institutional forms (Zelizer, 1988). The emphasis upon institutions as important sites for forming individuals' attitudes, beliefs, values and systems of symbolic meaning also parallels the notion of 'mental models' used by Douglass North, where 'institutions are the external (to the mind) mechanisms that individuals create to structure and order the environment', and which evolve alongside their 'individual cognitive systems create[d] to interpret the environment' (North, 1994, p. 363).

'Old' and 'new' institutionalism

A distinction is often made between the 'old' and 'new' institutional economics (Dugger, 1990; Hodgson, 1993; Rutherford, 1994, 2001; Furubotn and Richter, 2005). The 'old' institutionalism is associated with the dissident tradition in economics that developed in the United States, associated with Thorstein Veblen, J. R. Commons, Clarence Ayres and J. K. Galbraith (Dugger and Sherman, 1994; Rutherford, 1994; Stilwell, 2002). Characteristic features of this institutionalist tradition are a stress upon power and conflict as inherent features of capitalist economies; a focus upon technologies as drivers of change that challenge existing institutional arrangements; and the need for economics to be both evolutionary in its approach and interdisciplinary in its method.

The intellectual founder of institutionalism was the American economist Thorstein Veblen. Veblen argued the necessity of an evolutionary perspective to understanding modern industrial economies; he also argued that neoclassical economics provided an inadequate foundation for understanding dynamic change. Veblen critiqued the focus of neoclassical economics on methodological individualism and rational choice, deriding its treatment of individuals as being hedonistic 'lightning calculators of pleasure and pain' (Veblen, 1961 [1909], p. 73). For Veblen, the assumption of methodological individualism meant that when institutions are 'involved in the facts with which the theory is occupied, such institutional facts are taken for granted, denied, or explained away' (Veblen, 1961 [1909], p. 73). By contrast, Veblen insisted on the primacy of institutions, and the forms of custom and habit with which they were associated, arguing that 'it is ... on individuals that the system of institutions imposes those conventional standards, ideals, and canons of conduct that make up the community's system of life' (Veblen, 1909 [1961], p. 38).

Malcolm Rutherford (2001, p. 174) has observed that 'for Veblen...institutions were more than mere constraints on individual action, but embodied generally accepted ways of thinking and behaving. Thus, institutions worked to mould the preferences and values of individuals brought up under their sway.' This was apparent in Veblen's analysis of consumption, where culturally derived notions of status and display demonstrated what Veblen termed 'conspicuous consumption', and the desire of the middle and working classes to emulate the behaviour of the super-rich 'leisure class'. In the sphere of production, Veblen saw an ongoing tension between what he termed the 'instinct of workmanship' and the 'predatory instinct' of business owners, which 'includes activities that enhance profit without adding to the productive capacity of the economy' (Stilwell, 2002, p. 213). The prevalence of the 'predatory instinct' in modern capitalism, and its associated propensity towards waste of resources, led Veblen to increasingly favour a managed capitalism, where the state would increasingly involve itself in economic planning in order to optimise the benefits of technological change. Stilwell has observed that, in general, institutionalists have tended to favour an economic system that remains largely capitalist but is nonetheless 'steered by the state'. In that respect, they are broadly situated in a political 'middle ground between conservative neoclassicals and revolutionary Marxists' (Stilwell, 2002, p. 217).

The institutional paradigm identifies 'power relationships based on enabling myths...[as] the most important relationships in society' (Dugger and Sherman, 1994, p. 103). In this respect, it has important parallels with the critical political economy approach to media, as identified by Robert Babe (1995) and Vincent Mosco (2009, pp. 52–53). The Canadian communications theorist Harold Innis sought to integrate institutional economics as pioneered by Veblen with communication theories. In *The Bias of Communication* (Innis, 1991 [1951]), Innis traced the historical relationship between communication technologies and the rise and fall of empires, proposing that different dominant modes of communication had a political and cultural bias towards time, custom and tradition, as in the case of print, or towards spatial expansion, novelty and a futures orientation, as with broadcast media (Carey, 1989). William Melody (1987) and Robert Babe (1995) have drawn attention to commonalities in the projects and methods of both Veblen and Innis, identifying Veblen as an economist whose 'attention afforded [to] institutions necessarily privileged communicatory processes as agents of social organisation and of social change' (Babe, 1995, p. 154), and Innis as a political economist who 'attempt[ed] a full integration of evolutionary economics and information and communication into a social science based institutional analysis' (Melody, 1987, p. 1322).

The institutionalist tradition is a rich one that cannot be recounted in full detail here (see Stilwell, 2002, pp. 209–48; Hodgson, 2004; Chavance, 2009, pp. 4–31; Kapp *et al.*, 2012 for summaries). An important figure to note is the American economist John Kenneth Galbraith. Galbraith argued that the development of 20th-century capitalism had reached a point where there was no longer a single market system, but rather a two-tier economy, where the market system co-existed with a planning system (Galbraith, 1973). The latter entailed the largest corporations now being part of a 'planning system', where they have a significant degree of control over prices, market demand, technological development and, through their influence over the political process, government policy and the conduct of the modern state. From this standpoint, Galbraith argued that traditional neoclassical economics could only understand small businesses and not this planning system; in those industries where monopoly or oligopoly was the norm. Moreover, Galbraith argued that contemporary mass media were critical to this corporate-led planning system, as they enabled corporations to 'guide' consumer preferences, so that the 'channelling of prodigious resources into commercial advertising and other sales promotion activities' enabled 'the preferred pattern of production [to shape] the pattern of consumption' (Stilwell, 2002, p. 233).

New institutional economics

New institutional economics (NIE) has its origins in neoclassical economics, but brings forth the need for a more grounded understanding of market behaviour that recognised limitations that arise from the 'lack of institutional content in the core of neoclassical theory' (Rutherford, 2001, p. 186). Langlois (1986) has observed that it has shared concerns with the older institutionalist tradition about static equilibrium modelling, the lack of connections between economics and other branches of the social sciences and moral philosophy and the need for a more historical and evolutionary dimension in understanding the dynamics of modern capitalist economies. As the Nobel Prize winning economist and NIE pioneer Ronald Coase put it, 'modern institutional economics should study man (*sic*) as he is, acting within the constraints imposed by real institutions. Modern institutional analysis is economics as it ought to be' (Coase, 1984, p. 231). At the same time, authors within the NIE approach have stressed their continuities with mainstream microeconomics and their differences with the earlier institutionalist approaches. Oliver Williamson (1975, p. 1) argued that NIE was 'for the most part ... complementary to, rather than a substitute for, conventional analysis', and Elinor Ostrom has argued that institutional analysts need to 'use the working assumptions of models developed to apply contemporary rational choice theory' (Ostrom, 2005, p. 101). In defining the new institutionalist perspective, Richard Langlois observed:

> The problem with ... many of the early Institutionalists is that they wanted an economics with institutions but without theory; the problem with many neoclassicists is that they want economic theory without institutions; what we should really want is both institutions and theory – not only ... economic theory informed by the existence of specific institutions, but also an economic theory of institutions.
>
> (Langlois, 1986, p. 5)

Bounded rationality and transaction costs

The NIE has focused upon two 'real world' limitations of neoclassical economics that point to the need for new approaches to understanding the economics of institutions. The first is that of *bounded rationality*. Bounded rationality refers to the proposition that, while individual behaviour can be intentionally rational, 'in practice ... all decision makers (entrepreneurs, consumers, politicians, etc.) act subject to imperfect information and limited cognition' (Furubotn and Richter, 2005, p. 556). The origins of the concept lie with the organisation theorist Herbert Simon, who observed that 'the capacity of the human mind for formulating and solving problems is very small compared to the size of the problems whose solution is required for objectively rational behaviour in the real world – or even for a reasonable approximation to such objective reality' (Simon, 1957, p. 198). Among the reasons for such boundaries to individual rationality are the significant costs attached to acquiring and processing information, and the limited ability of individuals to store, retrieve and utilise information; this was the basis of Friedrich von Hayek's (1973) notion of *evolutionary rationality*, where 'individuals are unable to know in advance ... the full consequences that their actions will bring about' (Kerstenetsky, 2000, p. 165). There is also the existence of systematic distortions in human perceptions or thinking, which include ideologies and belief systems, described by Douglass North as the 'mental models...that individual cognitive systems create to interpret the environment' (North, 1994, p. 363).

The second key limitation is that of *transaction costs*. When neoclassical economics refers to costs, it typically refers to production costs (the costs of producing goods and services) and opportunity costs (the costs of alternatives foregone), but not to transaction costs, or what Kenneth Arrow termed the 'costs of running the economic system' (quoted in Williamson, 1985, p. 19). The most significant transaction costs include search and information costs, bargaining and decision costs, supervision and enforcement costs and investment in social markets. Transaction costs can include market engagement costs, managerial transaction costs – particularly those involving employment contracts within firms – and political transaction costs, or the costs of maintaining political and legal institutions associated with the running of a polity and governing a political system. Such transaction costs arise out of uncertainty and imperfect information among market participants, but also relate to the frequency with which market transactions occur and the degree to which any particular transaction entails transaction-specific investments.

There is a particularly important subset of transactions that are characterised by *asset specificity*, where both the nature of the asset and its use are incompletely defined. An example is the hiring of skilled workers sought for particular roles that have attributes unique to that person, and where the role has been structured with an expectation that the particular individual can define the tasks involved. Media industries are rife with hiring practices that draw upon a – frequently intangible – concept of asset specificity, or what Caves (2000) terms the 'A list/B list' phenomenon.

In professions such as acting, music, writing, the visual arts and so on, there are high levels of unemployment and under-employment, and people deriving only subsistence incomes from their professional craft, but there are also superstars who not only draw incomes far in excess of even those of corporate managers, but who have a great deal of control over the creative products with which they are involved. Even in roles where there may not appear to be a great deal of difference in creative talent, such as reading the television news, there are vastly different salaries paid to different presenters. The corollary is that such workers are frequently engaged in *implicit contracting* with their employers, where such salaries are contingent upon achieving particular performance outcomes (programme ratings, music downloads, box office success etc.). 'Reputation' constitutes a performance metric that is highly resistant to metrics and measurement, but which becomes decisive in one's ability to secure ongoing work in the media industries. The role of implicit or relational contracts will be discussed further below.

The firm as a nexus of contracts

The assumptions of bounded rationality and positive transaction costs have implications for understanding the role of contracts and the nature of the firm. People interact with one another through a social network of legally binding and non-binding obligations entered into voluntarily or through compulsion. Contractual obligations are legally binding and arise from the need to safeguard against opportunistic behaviour. Opportunism is not necessarily fraud or deceit, but is rather what Williamson (1985, p. 47) referred to as 'self interest seeking with guile', enabled by general conditions of uncertainty, imperfect information and conditions of information asymmetry between transacting parties. Ex ante opportunism involves the problem of adverse selection, where one party has less information about the other party than that party has about either themselves or their product. A well-known example is the 'market for lemons' (Akerlof, 1970), where both good and bad second-hand cars ('lemons' being the term used for the latter) are being sold, and the seller has far more information than any prospective buyer about which are good and bad. Ex post opportunism is referred to as *moral hazard* where, after the conclusion of a contract, one party is better informed than the other, or their efforts in undertaking the contractual obligation are unobservable by the other. A much discussed case of moral hazard is the *principal-agent problem* as it pertains to ownership and management in the modern corporation, where the managers (agents) who are acting on behalf of the principals (shareholders) invariably have more information than the principals (owners), and cannot therefore be guaranteed to be acting in the best interests of the shareholders. For example, they may undertake activities which maximise their own salaries rather than returns on investment (Jensen and Meckling, 1976; Fama and Jensen, 1983).

Contracts are a complex and highly legalistic means of ensuring compliance, premised upon the assumption that relations between managers and employees are necessarily adversarial. Moreover, as the size of any organisation increases, the range and complexity of the contracts in which it can become involved grows at an increasing rate. This leads to one of the key insights of NIE, which is about the nature of the firm. NIE theorists understand the firm, not simply as the institutional site through which goods are produced but as a *nexus of contracts*.

Drawing on insights originally developed by Ronald Coase (1937), the firm is seen as economising on transaction costs in two respects. First, through vertical integration of activities across its supply chain, it can set relative prices within the corporation, drawing upon a common pool of corporate information. Second, through employment contracts, a single *incomplete contract* is substituted for many complex ones that reduce the cost of negotiating and concluding multiple contracts; such incomplete contracts can also be more readily adjusted for changing market circumstances (Williamson, 1975, p. 4). Subsequent development of Coase's work by Williamson (1975, 1985) has drawn attention to the importance of *relational contracts*, which are particularly important to employment contracts, but are also relevant to sub-contracting, producer/supplier relations and so on. A relational contract is necessarily incomplete, as it presumes that the specified transactions constitute only part of a wider structure of embedded relations, as there are personal dimensions to acquittal of the contract. The 'incomplete' nature of contracts draws attention to the degree to which these personal relations are commonly implicit, informal and non-binding, and actual performance hinges upon elements of self-motivation and self-monitoring (Furubotn and Richter, 2005, pp. 173–75).

Contracting complexity in the media

One prominent application of the New Institutional Economics to media, the arts and entertainment has been Richard Caves' *Creative Industries: Contracts Between Art and Commerce* (Caves, 2000). Caves argued that the creative industries could be defined not only by what they provided to the public, as 'industries supplying goods and services that we broadly associate with cultural, artistic, or ... entertainment value' (Caves, 2000, p. 1), but also by the pervasiveness of contracts in such industries. For Caves, the creative industries include book and magazine publishing, the visual and performing arts, music, cinema, TV and radio, fashion and games. Other accounts have also included advertising, architecture, design industries, galleries and museums and computer software as being among the creative industries (Flew, 2012).

Caves identifies seven economic properties of the creative industries which meant that 'creative goods and services, the processes of their

(Continued)

production, and the preferences and tastes of creative artists differ in substantial and systematic ... ways from their counterparts in the rest of the economy' (Caves, 2000, p. 2). These include:

1. Endemic uncertainty about consumer demand, arising from the 'experience good' qualities of creative works;
2. Creative workers who care greatly about both their work and product and are prepared to accept relatively lower incomes as a trade-off for pleasurable forms of work;
3. The requirement of a diverse array of skills to produce a complex creative good or service;
4. Infinitely differentiated creative products;
5. The existence of a 'star system' and vertically differentiated skills in terms of how they are valued in the market ('A list' actors, superstar artists, etc.);
6. The need to complete complex projects, with a 'motley crew' of creative and other workers, within particular time frames, as maximisation of demand is often time-dependent (e.g. getting movies aimed at children out in time for the Christmas holidays);
7. The durability of creative products, and the ability of the most successful creative works to maintain value over time, as reflected in the legal duration of copyright and the payment of royalties.

Contracts in the creative industries may be simple or complex. For a particular artist producing a creative work for sale (e.g. a painter, writer or musician), the relationship with the various industry 'gatekeepers' (agents, publishers, distributors, gallery owners etc.) may constitute a simple or one-off contractual arrangement. But even in this instance, if creative workers envisage a career in this field, they will develop more complex relationships, as various cultural intermediaries will decide whether the prospective value of their creative output warrants the ongoing investment of 'humdrum' inputs required to place their work before prospective buyers. In exchange, such cultural intermediaries will receive a share of future royalties deriving from sales of the artist's creative work.

Complex projects are those requiring 'the collaboration of several parties, each providing different but complementary inputs or resources' (Caves, 2000, p. 12). Contracts address several issues in

(Continued)

organising the production of complex cultural goods such as a feature film, a computer game or a television programme. They provide a means of managing incentives in complex team-based production processes, where the contribution of any individual participant is difficult to measure, but all participants have incentives to produce the product best able to capture commercial returns. Incentive contracts (e.g. those where participants secure a percentage of gross revenues on release) are one means of addressing this, most likely to be deployed for 'star' inputs; for others, implicit contracts are typically in operation, which rely upon the value that each participant places on their reputation, and ability to secure future work on that basis. Caves followed Coase and Williamson in identifying the firm as a 'nexus of contracts', whereby some creative workers become employees and are subject to employment contracts within the firm, but where a significant number of creative workers instead rely upon more complex individual contracts that are tied to particular projects or industry clients.

The NIE approach understands the firm as a *governance structure* through which 'order can be brought to relations that might otherwise lead to conflict and lost opportunities for mutual gains' (Furubotn and Richter, 2005, p. 180). *Governance structures* within firms thus constitute a complex and variable mix of market governance, self-governance, bilateral governance (e.g. management/worker relations, supplier/producer relations) and governance through third parties and collective agencies (e.g. lawyers, regulators, trade unions). Such governance activities occur under the general conditions of asset specificity, uncertainty arising from bounded rationality and information costs, the possibility for opportunistic behaviour and transactions with differing degrees of frequency (Williamson, 1985, pp. 72–80). The result is that firms need to be understood as complex organisations with their own cultures and governance structures, and not simply as 'black boxes' through which production occurs and profits are maximised subject to resource constraints. This conception of firms as being constituted by *dense networks of relational contracts* is seen as having wider application to 'all types of organisations, small and large...effective relational contracts can be said to hold in market relationships, firms, non-profit institutions, government bodies, government enterprises, and so on' (Furubotn and Richter, 2005, p. 190).

Institutions, governance structures and the institutional environment

NIE defines institutions as 'the humanly devised constraints that structure human interaction' (North, 1994, p. 360) and understands them in two senses. First, there are *institutional arrangements* or governance structures through which resources are allocated within particular organisations (the microscopic level); this is the level of the firm or organisation, as discussed above. Second, there is the *institutional environment* (macroscopic level), or the 'rules of the game in a society, or...the humanly devised constraints that shape human interaction' (North, 1990, p. 3). Within the institutional environment, a further distinction is made between *formal institutions*, which include rules, laws, constitutions, allocations of property rights and so on, and *informal constraints*, such as norms of behaviour, conventions and self-imposed codes of conduct (North, 1994, pp. 360–62; Williamson, 2000, pp. 596–99). While both form the 'rules of the game' through which particular forms of action are either encouraged (through incentives) or discouraged (through laws, constraints and punishments), formal institutions are more amenable to substantive change – through concerted political action, for example – than the more historically and culturally embedded informal constraints. North gives the example of the former communist states of Russia and Eastern Europe to indicate how simply transferring the formal rules of one system to another, in this case the Western system of private property rights, did not in itself transform economic performance as it had only a limited impact on the informal norms of these societies (North, 1994, p. 366).

Williamson (2000) has proposed that NIE understands the economics of institutions as operating across four interconnected layers which have their own discrete historical temporalities and analytical methods: (1) historically and culturally embedded informal institutions, customs, traditions, norms and values, and what North referred to as 'mental maps', incorporating cognitive processes and belief systems; (2) the formal institutional environment, as manifested in constitutions, laws, bureaucracy, political institutions and so on, and the credibility such governing institutions have among market participants; (3) governance structures pertaining to contracts and the management of transaction costs within and between organisations; and (4) market

Table 3.1 Levels of analysis in the new institutional economics

Level of theory	Level of analysis	Frequency of change	Purpose
Level 1 Social theory	Embeddedness; 'mental maps'; informal institutions, customs, traditions, norms, religion, belief systems	100–1000 years	Often non-calculative; spontaneous
Level 2 Economics of property rights/law and politics	Institutional environment; formal rules of the games – esp. property (polity, judiciary, bureaucracy); credibility of governing institutions	10–100 years	Getting institutional environment right; 1st order economising
Level 3 Transaction cost economics	Governance; play of the game – esp. contracts (aligning governance structures with transactions)	1 to 10 years	Getting governance structures right; 2nd order economising
Level 4 Neo-classical economics	Resource allocation and employment (prices and quantities; incentive alignment)	Continuous	Getting marginal conditions right; 3rd order economising

Source: Williamson (2000). Reproduced with permission of Oliver E. Williamson and the American Economic Association.

transactions, which are best explained through neoclassical economic theories (Table 3.1).

So what new insights can be derived from such work in relation to studying the media? We will consider policy implications in more detail later in the chapter, but a couple of observations can be made. One is scepticism about the real market power of media giants, albeit for different reasons to those identified in neoclassical media economics. Whereas neoclassical theories have identified the continuing influence of the media mogul as a basis for sub-optimal decisions about running a media business, due to a mix of personal vanities and the desire for political influence (e.g. Knee *et al.*, 2009), NIE theorists identify the separation of asset managers from shareholders, or principal-agent problems, as being a particular problem in media industries. Richard Caves (2000) argued that managers of large media businesses commonly believe that they can capture elusive economic rents by controlling a diverse portfolio of businesses in activities related to their core business: the success of the Disney entertainment corporation is often cited as the ideal case study of the successful exploitation of such 'synergies'. But in practice many of these conglomeration strategies have failed to deliver the promised returns to shareholders, not least because they sought to merge incompatible corporate cultures. Caves suggests that the gains from conglomeration in the media industries are most commonly captured by managers themselves, who can gain salary bonuses from evidence of corporate expansion, and by star artists who can draw upon the resulting buzz to negotiate better contracts. Shareholders, as the ultimate owners of these companies, are frequently left worse off as a result of such expansionary strategies, meaning that, as *The Economist* put it, 'when media giants start talking about synergies, run to the hills' (cited in Flew, 2011a, p. 99).

Another distinctive element of NIE thinking has been around the nature of government regulation, and particularly the potential for *regulatory capture* of public agencies by the private sector industries they regulate. In his critique of the Federal Communications Commission (FCC), Ronald Coase (1959) challenged the notion that the FCC was primarily motivated by 'public interest' concerns, instead arguing that

> however fluid an organization may be in its beginning, it must inevitably adopt certain policies and organisational forms which condition its thinking and limit the range of its policies ... the regulatory commission may search for what is in the public interest, but it is not likely to find acceptable any solutions which imply fundamental changes in its settled policies.
>
> (Coase, 1966, p. 442)

For Coase, this was not in itself evidence of a conspiracy, although one of its consequences had been the preservation of oligopolistic market structures and monopoly profits in the broadcast media industries. Instead, it was argued that it is difficult to operate closely with an industry without coming to look at its problems in industry terms...the commission, although thinking of itself as apart from and with different aims from the industry, will nonetheless be incapable of conceiving of or bringing about any radical changes in industry practices or structure.

(Coase, 1966, p. 442)

In a line of argument that would have considerable influence among those promoting broadcasting deregulation in the 1980s and 1990s, Coase concluded that 'the regulation of the broadcasting industry by the Federal Communications Commission resembles a professional wrestling match. The grunts and groans resound throughout the land, but no permanent injury seems to result' (Coase, 1966, p. 442). We will return to the concept of regulatory capture in discussing policy implications of institutional analyses in the latter part of this chapter.

Economic sociology

In contrast to economics, the formal study of institutions has long been a feature of sociological research (Smelser and Swedberg, 2005). Founding figures in sociology such as Emile Durkheim viewed institutions as the symbolic systems – systems of belief and collective representations – that bound individuals to a social order (Scott, 2008, pp. 11–12). For Durkheim, the laws of contract which underpinned market transactions were themselves the product of norms and conventions, and a presumed moral order in society that provided the basis of such laws: 'wherever a contract exists, it is dependent on regulation which is the work of society not that of individuals' (Durkheim, 1964, p. 194). In the work of Max Weber, institutions are the historically formed structures which shape different national capitalisms, meaning that an 'ideal type' of the capitalist market economy has to be qualified in practice by recognition of the diversity of ways in which institutional mechanisms for enabling cooperation and managing conflict have evolved. In his book *The Great Transformation* (Polanyi, 1957), Karl Polanyi considered the risks presented by modern capitalism, where market relations become increasingly disembedded from social institutions and non-economic, or traditional, sources of institutional authority, such as the state, community-based institutions and informal institutions such as the family. Polanyi's work has greatly influenced economic sociology, since it proposes that 'because markets depend on non-economic conditions they can never be completely self-regulating... [and] economic behaviour is enmeshed in non-economic institutions' (Dale, 2010, p. 193).

Max Weber's *Economy and Society* (Weber 1978 [1922]) has been a formative text in economic sociology. In this book, Weber distinguished between 'pure economic action' – the one-off and everyday market transactions that economists study – and 'social economic action', which is oriented towards other social actors and occurs on a repeated basis. 'Social economic action' is seen as the proper domain of economic sociology, as such actions are influenced by a mix of custom and habit, convention and instrumental interests (Weber 1978 [1922], pp. 29–36).

Economic relationships can in turn be open or closed, and the basis of such relationships may be 'communal', or driven by a shared sense of belonging, or 'associative', and held together by mutual self-interest. Property relations are closed and associative, existing only between parties to a contract and driven by self-interest. Labour relations within a firm, however, have elements that are both communal and associative, as workers view themselves as being part of larger collective entities (guilds, unions, communities etc.), and such relations are tied together by power relations and institutional arrangements within a firm, as well as by mutual self-interest (Weber 1978 [1922], pp. 38–43; Swedberg, 2003, pp. 15–16).

What emerges from Weber's analysis is a typology of economic organisations, or sites where actors pursue purposive behaviour invested with some meaning towards other actors. These include: (1) primarily economic organizations, such as firms; (2) organisations that engage in economic activities even if that is not their primary purpose (e.g. churches, universities); (3) organisations which regulate economic activities (e.g. trade unions); and (4) those organisations which police the economic system (e.g. parliament, judiciary, government economic agencies) (Swedberg, 2003, p. 15–17).

Weber's work also emphasised the historically and institutionally differentiated forms that capitalism took. At its simplest, capitalism is defined as a system where profit is the primary motivator of economic action, and individuals are oriented towards 'opportunities for seeking new power of control over goods on a single occasion, repeatedly, or continuously' (Weber, 1978 [1922], p. 90). However, as Swedberg (2003, p. 59) observes, Weber's account of capitalism differs from that of Marx on the one hand and neoclassical economics on the other, in: (1) referring to capitalisms in the plural, rather than capitalism as a single unified system; (2) understanding different forms of capitalism as arising out of social action, rather than as consequences of a system with its own underlying laws and tendencies; and (3) developing historical typologies for different types of capitalism, as distinct from the Marxist focus on different modes of production.

Weber presented capitalism as being as much a form of social, institutional and moral order as it was a system based around markets and private property, as Swedberg has observed:

> The economic actor orients their behaviour not only towards other actors but towards 'orders', which consist of prescribed forms of social action that are enforced in different ways. These orders are sometimes institutions, and the central economic institution in modern capitalism is the rational enterprise, led by an entrepreneur and with a work force that is separated from the means of production. The economic order of private property is similarly defended and upheld in a predictable and reliable manner by the state and its administrative agencies. The legal system is part of the rational state and is similarly reliable and trustworthy. Huge investments in industry can be profitable only if the state authorities and the legal authorities are predictable in their decisions.
>
> (Swedberg, 2003, pp. 60–61)

Weber's historically defined capitalisms included: (1) rational capitalism, or capitalism as it first developed in Western Europe; (2) political capitalism, where profits arise out of a mix of force, corruption and clientelism; and (3) traditional capitalism, which remains primarily operated towards trade and commerce rather than industrial production. While Weber made much use of 'ideal types' in his analysis, his description of a 'rational' capitalist order should not be taken as an account of how capitalist economies actually function in reality. He noted, for instance, that 'rational' capitalism could be primarily oriented towards production and innovation, or towards finance and speculation, echoing observations made in different ways by Veblen and Keynes (Swedberg, 2003, p. 61). Weber is also often regarded as the pre-eminent theorist of bureaucracy, as he saw 'the increasing spread of bureaucracy as an inevitable accompaniment of the rationalised character of capitalist society' (Giddens and Held, 1983, p. 9). Importantly, Weber associated bureaucracy not only with the public sector but also with private corporations, observing that a 'bureaucratisation of capitalism' would see capitalist economies lose their entrepreneurial spirit and transformational drive (Weber, 1978 [1922], p. 999). As we note in the next chapter, such a concern also characterised the work of Joseph Schumpeter.

In sociology, there is a less clear 'break' between earlier traditions of institutional research and more recent developments in economic sociology than is the case with economics. *Network theories of organisations*, to take one example, have returned to earlier themes found in the work of Weber and Polanyi about the embeddedness of economic transactions in social relations, while drawing upon social network analysis to map such links (Convert and Heilbron, 2007; Scott, 2013). Mark Granovetter (1985) emphasised the importance of interpersonal relations and notions of trust in economic transactions, noting that 'the anonymous market of neoclassical models is virtually non-existent in economic life and transactions of all kinds are rife with social connections' (Granovetter, 1985, p. 495). He argued that 'social relations between firms are more important...than is supposed [and]...a balanced and symmetrical argument requires attention to power in "market" relations and social connections within firms' (Granovetter, 1985, p. 501). From an organisational perspective, W. R. Scott (2014) has drawn attention to three pillars through which institutions confer meaning to individuals and provide guides to social action:

1. *Regulative*: rules, laws, sanctions, formal governance frameworks and operating procedures that individuals comply with for essentially pragmatic reasons (costs/benefits);
2. *Normative*: values, norms, roles, conventions and binding expectations that provide frameworks of moral governance that both constitute informal constraints upon individuals and enable social obligations (rights/duties);
3. *Cultural-cognitive*: symbolic representations, systems of belief and shared frameworks for producing meaning that provide individuals with 'cultural rules establishing the logics of practice within a particular organisational context' (Scott, 2014, p. 76).

If we consider the latter cognitive-cultural dimension of institutions, we again find that the distinction between institutions and culture is often blurred, since both institutions and culture are based on habits of thought and behaviour that are grounded in everyday interactions with institutions (Dequech, 2003). In this respect, key economic institutions of capitalism, such as firms and markets, would be seen as cultural entities: the lines between economics and cultural analysis become fundamentally interconnected in such an approach.

Applications of institutional economics

In contrast to neoclassical media economics and political economy, there have been relatively few applications of institutional economics to the media industries. We have already discussed Richard Caves' work on relational contracts in the media industries, which draws extensively upon the NIE literature. We will next discuss the institutional bases of broadcast media property and global media policy as case studies in institutionalism, while noting some of the important differences between NIE theorists and economic sociologists on such questions. Further applications of institutional theories to the media, such as its ability to enhance understanding of public service broadcasting, will be discussed in Chapter 5.

Broadcasting property

Institutional analysis also provides insights into the role played by policy in shaping broadcasting property, and how economic principles are balanced with social and cultural factors. Virtually all governments have chosen to control the allocation of electromagnetic spectrum for purposes of radio and television broadcasting. In many countries this initially took the form of a state monopoly, while others adopted a mixed model (dual system) of commercial and public service broadcasting. In the United States, which is almost unique in allowing for an entirely commercialised model of broadcasting, the right to use the spectrum for such purposes was allocated through licencing, and control over a broadcasting licence entailed other obligations, particularly relating to media content. A similar approach was taken in other countries that had a dual system, such as Australia, Canada and – after an initial period of BBC monopoly – the United Kingdom (see Herd, 2012 for Australia).

In his account of the history of policies towards commercial broadcasting in the United States, Thomas Streeter (1996) argued that 'commercial broadcasting . . . is more a product of deliberate political activity than a lack of it'. He argued that commercial broadcasting is 'political, not just in the sense that it requires spectrum regulation and similar regulatory activities, but because its . . . commercial [organisation] . . . is itself dependent on extensive and ongoing collective activities'. As a result, 'the effort to create a free open marketplace has produced an institution that is dependent on government privileges and other forms of collective constraints' (Streeter, 1996, pp. xii–xiii).

(Continued)

Streeter's account stresses the hybrid nature of market/state relations in broadcasting property, as seen in the history of commercial licences and the conditions that have been attached to them. Herd (2012) has similarly argued that an adequate understanding of Australian commercial television history requires an institutional account that draws attention to the importance of policy developments in shaping the path-dependent evolution of the broadcasting networks. Herd proposed that Australian commercial television has since its inception in the 1950s constituted an institutional field where 'government... plays a central role in such things as property rights, rules of exchange and rules of governance' (Herd, 2012, p. x).

Broadcast media licensing departs from standard property rights allocation in three critical ways. The three core rights associated with physical property are: (1) the right to own and use an asset; (2) the right to derive income from an asset; and (3) the right to use an asset as one sees fit as an owner, including the right to dispose of that asset or to change the ways in which it is being used (Williamson, 1985, p. 27; Furubotn and Richter, 2005, p. 87). The allocation of broadcast licences has modified these three core property rights in key ways:

1. Governments have mandated the number of broadcast licences that can operate in a single geographical area, which in practice has made it illegal to set up a new competitor in that area. While this was historically justified in terms of competing uses of scarce spectrum space, it has continued to set barriers to entry for new competitors long after the original technical rationale ceased to be relevant (Horwitz, 1989; Christensen, 2011);
2. The holding of a broadcast licence has been taken to be part of a wider 'public trust' obligation that owners have to the wider community, which has entailed restrictions on who can or cannot own a broadcast licence. These include local ownership requirements, minority ownership preferences, restrictions on foreign ownership and limits to cross-media ownership (e.g. a newspaper owner may be prevented from acquiring a broadcasting licence in a particular area) (Horwitz, 1989, pp. 154–67);
3. The holders of broadcasting licences have been subject to a variety of content and standard obligations concerning what they put to air. These can include requirements relating to national content quotas, requirements to broadcast locally produced material

(Continued)

and obligations pertaining to children's programming, fairness in news and current affairs and provision for cultural and linguistic minorities (van Cuilenberg and McQuail, 2003).

One of the earliest critics of such arrangements in broadcasting was the University of Chicago economist Ronald Coase. In an early application of new institutional economics, Coase (1959, 1966) argued for a greater role for markets in allocating property rights in spectrum, seeing the current system as producing regulated oligopolies that limited consumer choice in broadcasting. The critiques of broadcasting regulation by Coase and others greatly influenced movements worldwide to deregulate broadcasting industries from the 1970s onwards. In the United States, it was associated with championing the cable television sector as providing programming alternatives to terrestrial broadcasting, and while there certainly was expanded consumer choice in US television, a new problem emerged of cable service providers holding monopoly rights in local areas and, not surprisingly, using such network control to ramp up subscription fees to consumers (Streeter, 1996, pp. 174–81).

For sociologists such as Streeter, this confirms how attempts to isolate property rights from political influence are likely in practice to fail as they begin from flawed first premises, and that since the allocation of property rights has a governmental dimension, it is appropriate for media reformers to use that as leverage to shape media in terms of their political and socio-cultural roles. More generally, deregulation in media industries such as broadcasting and telecommunications was typically followed by re-regulation, and the introduction of new principles to safeguard the 'public interest' in more competitive markets. This was partly because those disadvantaged by new arrangements sought action from elected governments to address their concerns. It was also because more competition itself created pressures towards new forms of monopoly, as with the case of cable companies discussed above, and government action itself turned out to be a requirement for the maintenance of competitive behaviour and freedom of entry into new markets (Christensen and Laegreid, 2011).

NIE theorists and economic sociologists share the view that broadcasting represents a case where governments have actively involved themselves in the allocation of property rights that in turn shape the ways in which markets operate in these industries. For economic sociologists such as Roy (2004, pp. 437–39), broadcasting exemplifies three core assumptions about corporations and property rights: (1) that specific rights, entitlements and obligations are variable rather than fixed; (2) that property is a social relationship, and that the maintenance of property rights is likely to have a political dimension; and (3) that the existence and maintenance of particular property rights actively involves the state and its agencies. In this instance, the stability of broadcast licencing arrangements over time is partly the result of the political power and effective lobbying efforts of the incumbent broadcasters, but also reflects the extent to which other interests have benefited from restrictions on market competition. In the Australian case, for example, monopoly profits from the incumbent broadcasters have ensured an adequate stream of revenues to invest in Australian programme production, including children's and local drama production, and have thus tended to have the support of unions and cultural advocates in the television sector (Flew, 2006).

By contrast, NIE theorists view such outcomes with concern and ask 'whether mistaken property rights assignments were responsible for resource misallocations' (Williamson, 1985, p. 27). They can be seen to exemplify rent seeking, which involves 'the expenditure of scarce resources to change existing legal and other constraints so that monopoly rents can be captured' (Furubotn and Richter, 2005, p. 566). NIE theorists have argued that since 'specific institutional constraints dictate the margins at which organisations operate and hence make intelligible the interplay between the rules of the game and the behaviour of actors' (North, 1990, p. 110), such restrictions 'generate perverse incentives... and give rise to property rights that discourage innovation and private entrepreneurship' (Nee, 2005, p. 51). In particular, the bureaucratic allocation of broadcast property rights is seen as generating incentives on the part of incumbent broadcasters to engage in political lobbying to protect the status quo, rather than investing in better quality programming as they would have to in the face of a more competitive market environment. As a result, these economists have tended to favour a deregulatory approach, promoting reduced obligations upon the property rights of incumbent broadcasters, the entry of new competitors into existing markets and the promotion of new technologies and services (Christensen, 2011). In that respect, they characteristically see 'public trust' obligations as a ruse for 'rent seeking' behaviour and indicative of the capture of regulators and legislators by incumbent interests.

In the wake of significant deregulation in both broadcasting and telecommunications worldwide since the 1980s, we are now in a position to concretely assess the relative claims of these competing approaches to media regulation. The NIE critique of regulatory agencies as being 'captured' by those industry players they regulate, and the resulting propensity to enable rent-seeking behaviour by restricting market entry, drew attention to problems with the prevalent 'public interest' understanding of regulation (Horwitz, 1989; Baldwin and Cave, 2012; Lunt and Livingstone, 2012). One was a degree of fuzziness around the question of whether regulatory agencies are intended to be the politically neutral administrators and deliverers of policies dictated by the elected representatives of the day, or whether governments can expect to be able to work with, and take advice from, regulatory agencies in pursuit of agreed policy objectives (Lunt and Livingstone, 2012, pp. 21–22).

While these principles are not inevitably incompatible, they do raise the issue of the relationship of regulators to the policy process, which is also raised by the question of whether their role is to facilitate dialogue between competing interest groups in a particular policy sphere, in order to get outcomes that reflect a compromise between these competing interests. It is in this sense that NIE critics such as Coase and other 'public choice' theorists identified a key flaw in pluralist models of the policy process – they assumed that the 'public interest' was broadly reflected by competing interest groups, thereby losing sight of those who do not collectively organise to access public resources or favourable policy treatment (Dunleavy and O'Leary, 1987, pp. 159–63; Baldwin and Cave, 2012, pp. 43–49). In the broadcasting sphere, for instance, it was argued that the 'fiction' of spectrum scarcity had privileged incumbent media outlets at the expense of potential new competitors, with the unintended consequence of reducing consumer choice of media content below what it may otherwise have been.

At the same time, over three decades of deregulation has clarified what are some of the limitations of policies pursued towards this end. One is that measures to promote greater competition, or the privatisation of public assets, have frequently led to more regulation, rather than less, as various policy trade-offs that may have once been internalised within large corporations (e.g. universal service obligations in telecommunications) now become the responsibility of government agencies required to adjudicate on competing claims. A number of theorists of regulation refer to the rise of the *regulatory state* whose tasks have become more complex and multi-faceted over the period since the 1980s (e.g. Braithwaite, 2008; Baldwin and Cave, 2012, pp. 373–87). Moreover, regulation is no longer simply a matter of government agencies implementing command-and-control regulations over private entities. There now exist a complex array of regulatory forms, including co-regulation, self-regulation, incentives-based regulation and 'nudge' approaches to changing corporate and consumer behaviour (Freiberg, 2010). There is also evidence of the failures of deregulation, including the commonly – but not universally – accepted view that reduced scrutiny over the conduct of financial institutions in the United States, the United Kingdom and elsewhere was a major contributing factor to the Global Financial Crisis of 2008 (e.g. Stiglitz, 2010). In their account of contemporary thinking about regulation, Baldwin and Cave conclude that discussions have been moving beyond 'the virtues and vices of deregulation and privatisation' towards

> newer conversations about regulation [where] it has become accepted, not only that regulation is necessary for the functioning of a market economy, but that regulatory oversight remains essential in the running of public services, especially those involving naturally monopolistic elements.... An initial emphasis on economic regulation that was supposed to 'wither away' over time has been replaced by a realization that there is a continuing need for regulatory oversight and an imperative to add environmental and sustainability objectives to the earlier, primarily economic and social, objectives.
>
> (Baldwin and Cave, 2012, pp. 9–10)

Global media policy

A final case study of new institutional economics can be seen in the analysis of international audiovisual media policy institutions, and global media policy more generally, undertaken by Jan Loisen (2012). Institutionalism has a long history in international relations theory, as it has been associated with the realist paradigm (Gilpin, 2002). Realists identify the paradox of the continuing growth of international institutions, despite their apparent inability to exercise power over nation-states without the support of other nation-states. It is argued that the ideas associated with multilateralism align with the interests of nation-states when the latter identify a collective interest in establishing common rules of the game, so as to provide greater

(Continued)

certainty – or, in the language of NIE, to reduce transaction costs – associated with cross-border trade, investment and other activities. An interest in institutions is not, however, restricted to any one school of international political economy. Ruggie (1992) observes that multilateral institutions exist as both formal institutions 'with headquarters and letterheads, voting procedures, and generous pension plans' and as ideas about the benefits of cooperation among states that take shape around both formal and informal constraints which promote 'institutionalised behaviour, defined by...generalised principles of conduct' (pp. 573, 574).

Loisen draws upon North's distinction between institutions and organisations, or the rules of the game and the players in the game, in observing that 'the goal of the rules is to define how the game is to be played. Regulated by the institutional framework, the players try to win the game through aptitude, strategy, coordination, or even foul play' (Loisen, 2012, p. 37). Key to the NIE understanding of effective institutions is the idea of credible commitments, or the existence of third parties prepared to both enforce rules agreed to by contracting parties and accept that formal and informal rules in turn set constraints upon their own behaviour. The international trading framework, as a set of binding contracts that have been agreed to by multiple parties, aims to secure such credible commitments. The ability of the international trading framework to do so is shaped by 'a mix of ideological factors (in the form of ideas and examples), interests (as defined by politics and economics), and institutions (as they shape constraints and opportunities)' (Bhagwati, 1993, p. 17). Institutions can thus be seen as a linking system in the 'Three I's' of ideas, institutions and interests:

> The various ideas and power dynamics shape institutions, aiming to reduce uncertainty and to structure interaction.... The institutional framework is also a determinant of what perceptions will matter and how these will be translated into transforming the environment.
>
> (Loisen, 2012, p. 45)

Applying this framework to international audiovisual media policy, Loisen (2012, p. 48) proposes that there are three relevant levels of governance:

(Continued)

1. The institutional framework that applies to audiovisual trade, which includes the General Agreement on Trade in Services (GATS), organisations such as the World Trade Organisation (WTO) and UNESCO and relevant civil society organisations such as public broadcasters and commercial media companies. Embedded within this institutional framework include ideas that are in conflict (e.g. culture as tradable commodity/culture as national cultural identity), as well as particular cases where enforcement has occurred;
2. The wider WTO institutional framework, including the GATS, particular cases that have been before the WTO, ideas about international governance (e.g. liberalism, realism, nationalism, internationalism) and the full range of actors both within and outside of the relevant international agencies;
3. The totality of forms of international economic policy governance.

Each of these three levels can be analysed across the four quadrants that can be derived from North's work:

1. Informal constraints: ideas about international governance and reciprocity between trading parties;
2. Formal rules: international trade laws, rules, treaties, agreements and conventions;
3. Enforcement of formal rules;
4. Organisations and actors with international governance responsibilities (Figure 3.1).

For Loisen, one of the merits of the NIE framework is that 'it can result in a narrative that allows competing evaluations to be tied together and explored further' (Loisen, 2012, p. 47). At one level, the case of audiovisual policy would appear to indicate the failure of multilateralism under the GATS agreement. A large number of nations, including all European Union member states, have chosen to exempt their audiovisual industries from the most-favoured nation (MFN) principle, meaning that 'the scope to retain a locally or nationally defined audiovisual policy that makes use of trade barriers can be maintained' (Loisen, 2012, p. 47). Moreover, the entry

(Continued)

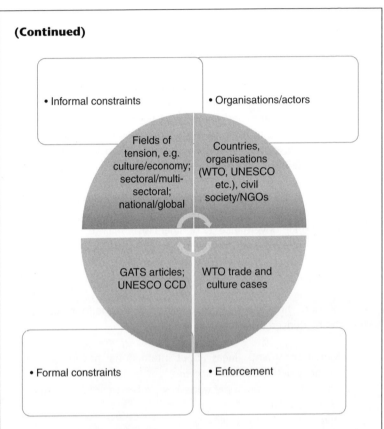

Figure 3.1   Mapping the institutional framework of global audiovisual media policy
Source: Loisen (2012, p. 48). Reproduced with permission of Intellect Books.

of UNESCO into such debates with the adoption of the Convention on Cultural Diversity (CCD) by 132 member states (including the European Union) would appear to provide protection for national cultural policies, acting as a countervailing force to trade liberalisation and the WTO.

But Loisen argues that such accounts underestimate the extent to which GATS provisions remain legally enforceable, whereas exemptions from the GATS, or appeal to conventions such as the CCD, 'provide hardly any clarity, legal certainty or strengthened support for cultural diversity' (Loisen, 2012, p. 49). The GATS agreement is

---

(Continued)

also not only a formal constraint but an informal one: it has changed the 'rules of the game' in global media policy in ways that generate a path-dependent momentum to trade liberalisation that is not necessarily dependent upon the formal enforcement powers of the WTO. Moves towards bilateral trade agreements that incorporate free trade in audiovisual services are one way in which ideas and interests can be aligned without necessary dependence upon particular institutions, as is the tendency of convergence to merge audiovisual media with other communications policy arenas where cultural arguments have less provenance such as telecommunications.

Conclusion

In this chapter, we have considered the contribution of institutional economics in the context of more general institutionally oriented approaches in the social sciences. The study of institutions sits between approaches primarily informed by methodological individualism and those that emphasise the determining role of social structures. We have drawn attention to the path-dependent history of institutions and the nature of institutions as formal organisations, as 'rules of the game' and as informal constraints. We have also identified the mutually shaping interactions between individuals and institutions, and the paradox of institutions existing independently of the individuals within them, yet having an important role in shaping the 'mental maps' of individuals and how they think about the world and their place within it. It was noted that there exist historical, sociological and rational choice variants of institutionalism, with the latter being particularly important within economics, and at the core of the NIE.

There exists a traditional institutional economics that has developed in opposition to neoclassical economics around questions of power and conflict, the cultural forces that shape individuals in society, and the need for an evolutionary and interdisciplinary perspective in understanding modern economies. By contrast, the NIE emerged as an outgrowth of conventional economic analysis, identifying bounded rationality and transaction costs as two important drivers of the formation of economic institutions, and understanding the modern firm as a nexus of formal and relational contracts, subject to a diverse array of internal and external governance structures.

While NIE has developed a means of understanding historical and institutional change, important questions remain about the extent to which it remains within the *corpus* of conventional neoclassical economics, or whether it will more fruitfully develop in alignment with other approaches to the study of institutions, such as economic sociology. It was noted that Max Weber remains an important influence on understandings of capitalism as a complex institutional system, particularly in the attention that his work gave to the socio-legal 'rules of the game' and 'credible commitments' of capitalist economies, as well as the diversity of historical and institutional forms through which capitalist societies could evolve.

The chapter has outlined three case studies of applied institutionalism in media studies. The first concerned the role played by contracts in the economic co-ordination of complex forms of cultural production such as feature films, television programmes and digital video games. Second, the particular status of broadcast property as an outcome of regimes of governance was considered, where public regulation and market interactions are not at opposite ends of the spectrum, but rather are interlinked through the ways in which governments have allocated property rights in relation to broadcast media activities. Finally, there was consideration of the role played by supranational institutions such as the World Trade Organisation and legally binding agreements such as the General Agreement on Trade in Services on national audiovisual media policies.

The status of culture in institutional economics remains an important and somewhat unresolved question. On the one hand, institutions are themselves cultural, in that they confer meaning to individuals and provide guides to social action not only in the regulatory sense of rules, laws and sanctions, but in the normative sense of generating roles, expectations and codes for moral governance and in the cognitive sense of providing symbolic representations and shared interpretative frameworks that inform how individuals think within particular institutional and organisational structures. If this is the case, then all forms of economic activity are imbued with a cultural dimension, from market behaviour to the relative importance of acquisitive and altruistic instincts in individual conduct.

The NIE has been resistant to going this far in a *rapprochement* with economic sociology and related fields, as it negates core neoclassical concepts of methodological individualism and rational choice. Rather, NIE theorists retain a more critical perspective on the ways in which property rights are assigned in different economies, seeing the key to changing both individual and organisational behaviour as residing primarily in the transformation of institutional structures. In this respect, NIE theories tend to take a more market-oriented approach to media economics than would be characteristic of other disciplines making use of institutional approaches to understanding media industries and markets. This has included viewing public sector agencies as engaging in self-interested regulatory behaviour as in the Coasian tradition. It can be noted, however, that contemporary debates about market regulation have been going beyond the couplet of regulation versus deregulation, towards greater awareness of the multiple tools, objectives and institutional arrangements through which the regulation of media markets can occur in contemporary capitalist economies.

4 Evolutionary Economics

This chapter outlines some of the contributions that evolutionary economics might make to media economics. Before we look at the sub-discipline of evolutionary economics and its potential media applications, however, we should confront head-on why evolutionary frameworks have rarely been taken up in the humanities.

Who's afraid of evolution?

The notion of biological evolution was developed in the mid-19th century, principally by Charles Darwin. Darwin's great book, *On the Origin of Species by Means of Natural Selection*, was published in 1859. Evolutionary economics is greatly indebted to Darwin, but works from the premise that the evolutionary mechanism, or algorithm, of differentiation, selection and amplification that generates diversity, adaptability and fitness for use is not only at work in the biological domain. This has been stated most dramatically by evolutionary economist Stan Metcalfe: 'Evolutionary theory is a matter of reasoning in its own right quite independently of the use made of it by biologists. They simply got there first' (1998, quoted in Hodgson and Knudsen, 2010, p. 1). From this, it also follows that, in the words of Sidney Winter, another of the key contributors to contemporary evolutionary economics, 'natural selection and evolution should not be viewed as concepts developed for the specific purposes of biology and possibly appropriable for the specific purposes of economics, but rather as elements of the framework of a new conceptual structure that biology, economics and other social sciences can comfortably share' (1987, quoted in Hodgson and Knudsen, 2010, p. 30).

While evolutionary theory has impacted many disciplines besides biology, including of course geology, but also psychology and archaeology, its implications have been downplayed, and sometimes strongly opposed, within the humanities because of the stain of social Darwinism and the approach to humanistic endeavour that would regard it as irreducible to an atavistic continuity with Nature. It is not possible in a book of this scope and focus to go into a detailed account of the debates around the adoption of evolutionary principles and analytical procedures in the social sciences and, latterly, the humanities.[1] However, it is important to address arguably the three most common and evident objections raised by humanists to the project that Hodgson and Knudsen (2010, p. 30) call 'generalising Darwinism'.

The first is the spectre of social Darwinism. A particularly crude direct application of Spencer's famous notion of 'survival of the fittest', particularly around questions of race, was developed in the late 19th century and then was consolidated in some versions of sociobiology in the 20th century. Given this history, resistance to generalising Darwinism has been especially strong in sociology, cultural anthropology and the humanities in general. But careful attention to Darwin's discussions of group selection, mutual aid, sympathy and cooperation should forestall 'individualist, uncritically pro-market, or other simplistic ideological notions that have sometimes been gathered under the misleading label social Darwinism' (Hodgson and Knudsen, 2010, p. 223). Research into human evolution, and its application into many disciplines, stresses the deeply, constitutively social nature of the human being. In *The Origin of Wealth: Revolution, Complexity, and the Radical Remaking of Economics*, Eric Beinhocker argues that 'the universality of strong reciprocity behaviour is staggering' (2006, p. 419). Contrary to the tabloid understanding of Darwinism as survival of the fittest being the equivalent of the devil take the hindmost, the current state of evolutionary biology and psychology affirms humans as *conditional cooperators* and *altruistic punishers*. Herbert Gintis and his colleagues define it as 'a predisposition to cooperate with others, and to punish (even at personal cost if necessary) those who violate the norms of cooperation' (Gintis *et al.*, 2005, p. 8).

This fundamental insight of the evolutionary sciences has been picked up by many disciplines. We see it close to the media, communication and cultural studies disciplines, for example, in Yochai Benkler's major work, *The Wealth of Networks* (2006). Benkler's research on the social affordances of digital networks emphasises the dynamic efficacy of cooperative, collective action: 'After years of arguments to the contrary, there is growing evidence that evolution may favour people who cooperate and societies that include such individuals' (Benkler, 2011, p. 79). There is now a very strong evolutionary evidence base that explains group solidarity, collective action and individual moral responsibility.

Evolutionary economics shares with neoclassical economics a firm regard for the efficiency with which markets distribute knowledge and perform hugely complex coordination functions from the bottom-up. Simply put, without markets working, by and large, as they do, societies as complex as ours not only could not work at all but would never have evolved to anywhere near their current state. But on the other hand, evolutionary economics knocks markets 'off their optimally efficient pedestal' (Beinhocker, 2006, p. 423). In concert with institutional economics, the evolutionary approach stresses the vast array of norms, customs, rules – what Arthur (2009) calls Social Technologies – that predate, surround, support, correct and limit the operations of markets.

The second objection concerns timescales for evolutionary change in the socioeconomic domain, as compared to the biological domain. According to Hodgson and Knudsen, in their systematic 'Search for General Principles of Social and Economic Evolution', there are six major information transitions in human history: (1) pre-linguistic culture; (2) human language; (3) tribal customs; (4) writing and records; (5) states and laws; and (6) the institutionalisation of science and technology. (Note the parallels to Weber's general history of economic societies discussed in Chapter 3.) The most recent major information transition – the institutionalised system of scientific and technological knowledge from the 17th century onwards – has 'multilevel ramifications' for socioeconomic evolution 'even if genetic evolution is negligible in the time span involved' (Hodgson and Knudsen, 2010, p. 233). In Brian Arthur's (2009) account, timescales for the evolution of technology and the coevolution of Social and Physical Technologies can take place, measurably, over decades.

The third objection concerns human agency and strategic intent. Evolution, in its classic biological formulation, is what Daniel Dennett (1995) calls a general-purpose algorithm for creating 'design without a designer'. However, socioeconomic evolution occurs out of the interplay, or coevolution, of physical technologies, social technologies (or institutions, as they have been presented in Chapter 3) and business strategy. 'Our intentionality, rationality, and creativity do matter as a driving force in the economy', Eric Beinhocker (2006, p. 15) notes, 'but they matter as part of a larger evolutionary process'.

Evolutionary economics

It has been a fundamental charge from the heterodox schools against neoclassical, or equilibrium, economics that it is not well equipped to account for change and growth. Whereas mainstream economics emphasises equilibrium, choice under conditions of scarcity and rational, utility-maximising agents, evolutionary economics stresses non-equilibrium processes that transform economies, firms, institutions, industries and employment *from within*. It treats processes of technological and institutional change and innovation not as exogenous shocks to an internally equilibrating system, but as endogenous to economies (Beinhocker, 2006). Such endemic change arises from the ceaseless activity of diverse agents with bounded rationality (a model of human behaviour much closer to observable reality than the neoclassical model of the 'utility maximising' individual).

Evolutionary economics offers a substantive alternative to neo-Marxist political economy and is based on a model of the effects, bad and good, of living under capitalism that is dynamic, conflict-driven and is explicitly indebted to Marxism (e.g. Catephores, 1994). This model is carried in the term 'creative destruction'. Creative destruction is 'a term originally derived from Marxist economic theory which refers to the linked processes of the accumulation and annihilation of wealth under capitalism' (http://en.wikipedia.org/wiki/Creative_destruction). The idea is powerful because it insists that 'accumulation' (progress, greater good for the greater number, etc.) and 'annihilation' (business failure, environmental degradation, etc.) are mutually constitutive forces. The term 'creative destruction' has become virtually synonymous with the work of Austrian-American economist Joseph Schumpeter since his major prognostications on the future of *Capitalism, Socialism, and Democracy* (1942).

For Schumpeter, like Marx, capitalism grows the seeds of its own downfall. But the seeds are not grown from its failure (the increasing immiseration of the masses, decreasing returns to scale, falling rate of profit) but from its success. Capitalism has delivered remarkable growth in the standard of living of working people, but the capitalist 'engine' drives incessant 'gales of creative destruction' – a metaphor uncannily like Marx's modernist *dictum* that 'all that is solid melts into air'. Over time, the culture that long-run capitalism breeds becomes inimical to it. Rationalisation and the erosion of bourgeois spiritual and moral values that gave capitalism its impetus, cost-benefit calculation made the benchmark of all manner of human transaction, the abstraction of stock market rather than real property relations, the routinisation of innovation: it all sounds like early, humanist, Marx 100 years on.

Capitalism, Socialism, and Democracy is Schumpeter's most enduring and influential work. It contains a sustained appreciation of Marx and one of the most searching systemic critiques of capitalism ever penned by one of its strongest defenders. Schumpeter argued that Marx had 'no adequate theory of enterprise' and failed to 'distinguish the entrepreneur from the capitalist' (quoted in McCraw, 2007, p. 349). According to his recent biographer Thomas McCraw (2007), Schumpeter 'told of capitalism in the way most people experience it: as consumer desires aroused by endless advertising; as forcible jolts up and down the social pecking order; as goals reached, shattered, altered, then reached once more as people try, try again'. He knew that 'creative destruction fosters economic growth but also that it undercuts cherished human values'. Admirers of Schumpeter think that he tells them what capitalism 'really feels like' (McCraw, 2007, p. 349).

There are both cataclysmic changes, such as the fundamental economic restructuring brought about by the advent of new general-purpose technologies and processes, and smaller, shorter-term business cycles. The big structural changes to economies were typically based on the Kondratieff–Schumpeter notion of long-wave cycles, of which there have been five since the Industrial Revolution: those based on (1) steam and cotton; (2) steel and railways; (3) chemistry and electrical engineering; (4) petrochemicals and cars; and (5) ICT. Some have proposed an expansion of the fifth or a new, sixth, wave consisting of biotech, pharmaceuticals, recycling and alternative energy, software, mobile communications and digital technology. The peak of the cycle is at the point at which existing technologies have been exploited fully, thereafter growth slows and only picks up again with a new generation of innovation.

Schumpeter emphasised that such change, both great and small, can be triggered by entrepreneurial effort which disrupts equilibrium, destroys established value and creates new value. Schumpeter's economics fell into obscurity during the long boom of Western post-war industrial growth and Keynesian social redistribution, but came back into prominence as the world searched for new models of growth in the wake of the 1970s oil shocks, stagflation and the decline of the Keynesian settlement. Innovation and entrepreneurialism became more of a watchword for post-industrial economies, and Schumpeter's 'second coming' has underpinned the development of contemporary innovation economics, which draws strongly on both institutional and evolutionary inputs (Freeman, 1987; Lundvall, 1988; Nelson, 1993; Edquist, 1997).

Contemporary evolutionary economics studies growth and change in economic systems under conditions of variety generation, enterprise competition and selection and self-organisation (see Metcalfe, 1998;

Loasby, 1999; Potts, 2000). Most of the empirical and theoretical work so far undertaken has focused on the manufacturing and high technology sectors, as have most analyses of the sources of innovation in contemporary economies. There is little yet that seeks to apply this new framework to the economic analysis of media, although some of the most interesting has focused on the broader question of innovation in services (Metcalfe and Miles, 2000; Boden and Miles, 2000). The core advance that this approach might facilitate is to understand creative industries, and particularly digital media, as an emergent, innovative part of the services sector of the economy (see Potts, 2011). The evolutionary approach places a focus on the ways economies *grow*, as complex open systems, rather than by optimising allocative efficiencies. It is also offer a clearer understanding of the way in which new technologies are integrated into an economy and the restructuring of organisations, industries, markets and consumer lifestyles the evolutionary growth can process requires.

An evolutionary account of media in the economy

An elaborated evolutionary account centred on media has been developed by Potts and Cunningham (2008). In keeping with the evolutionary emphasis on growth and change, this account of the contribution of creative industries, and particularly traditional and digital media, centres on their relative performance in relation to the economy as a whole. There are four models of this relationship: (1) negative – welfare, (2) neutral – competitive, (3) positive – growth and (4) emergent – innovation. Each of these hypotheses or models embodies a different account of value, a different policy response, and has been articulated across historically contingent circumstances which means they overlay each other. Each succeeds the previous but does not supersede it. In the first case a welfare subsidy is required; in the second, standard industry policy; in the third, investment and growth policy; and in the fourth, innovation policy is best (Table 4.1).

Model 1: The welfare model (special industry)

Model 1 is critical to cultural economics as it relates to the arts as well as to 'merit good' arguments for government support for certain types of media content and public service broadcasting. In it, the publicly supported arts and cultural heritage are hypothesised to have a

Table 4.1   Four models of the creative industries

Economic model	(1) Welfare	(2) Competitive	(3) Growth and (4) Innovation
Typical indicative content	Arts, crafts, material culture, heritage	'cultural industries': film, broadcasting, music, publishing	'creative industries': digital content, new, Internet and mobile media
Sub-discipline/ approach	Cultural economics	Neoclassical (descriptive)/ Political economy (critique)	Evolutionary economics/ innovation economics
Policy framework	Subsidy/grant	Industry policy	investment/ innovation

net negative impact on the economy, such that they consume more resources than they produce. To the extent that they continue to exist in a market economy, their value must lie at least in part beyond market value. In model 1, the arts and cultural heritage are essentially a 'merit good' sector that produces commodities that are welfare enhancing, but are only economically viable with a transfer of resources from the rest of the economy. The economic justification for allocative restitution ultimately rests on a *market failure* argument. Policy is then calibrated to estimates of this non-market value. If model 1 is true, then policy prescriptions should rightfully centre about income and resource reallocation, market or regulatory intervention, in order to protect an inherently valuable asset that is under threat in a market economy. Cultural Economics has largely been developed to address issues arising from these assumptions, and it is discussed in Chapters 1 and 5 in relation to PSM.

Model 2: The competitive model (just another industry)

Model 2 recognises that the established media (such as broadcasting, film and publishing) are mature business sectors: they are 'just another industry'. It presumes that the growth impact is neutral, such that these media contribute in aggregate no more or less technological change (origination of new ideas but also their adoption and retention) than the average of other sectors. If these media were at least as dynamic as other industries, then we should expect model 2 to be true.

Model 2 does not exclude the possibility that the economics of media are 'special', as in terms of extreme levels of demand uncertainty, power-law revenue models, tendencies towards monopoly, complex labour markets and property rights, endemic hold-up problems, information asymmetries, highly strategic factor markets and so on (e.g. Caves, 2000; De Vany, 2004). Their distinctive characteristics, however, can be addressed under established regulatory and market-competitive conditions. Model 2 thus thinks that, ultimately, these special features are no different to the special problems of most other industries, such as energy or tourism, which also have interesting features associated with scale, coordination, uncertainty or networks. The competitive model thus hypothesises that the established media will have industry performance statistics comparable to other sectors.

Model 3: The growth model (high-growth digital media and design as inputs into the broader economy)

Model 3 proposes a positive economic relation between high-growth digital media and design and growth in the aggregate economy. In this model, these forms of economic activity are one of the growth 'drivers' of contemporary economies, in a similar way agriculture was in the early 20th century, manufacturing was in the 1950s–60s and ICT was through the 1980s–90s. The possible reasons include that these activities introduce novel ideas into the economy that percolate to other sectors (e.g. new designs) or that they facilitate the adoption and retention of new ideas and technologies in other sectors (e.g. ICT). The key difference from models 1 and 2 is that in model 3 the creative industries are causally involved in the *growth* of the economy.

Evidence for this model would accrue from association of the creative industries with growth not just in jobs and commodities (as in model 2) but in *new* types of jobs and *new* sorts of commodities and services. This model accommodates design as an input factor into the economy, and interactive, mobile and Internet media. These exemplify input impact, such as games providing models for new generation education and learning paradigms or for simulation and virtual reality training in defence. It is evidenced by the positive correlation between design intensity in firms and their stock market performance. It also is evidenced by the growing proportion of creative occupations 'embedded' in the broader economy.

Model 4: The innovation model

Although these three models might seem exhaustive of analytic possibilities, a fourth model is also possible as an emergent dimension. Rather than thinking of the creative industries as an economic subset 'driving' growth in the whole economy, as in model 3, the creative industries may not be well characterised as a sector per se, but rather as an element of the *innovation system* of the whole economy. The economic value of the creative industries, in this view, is not in terms of their relative contribution to market values (as in models 1–3), but due to their contribution to the coordination of new ideas or technologies and thus to the process of change.

The creative sector, the hypothesis goes, lies at the heart of such innovation systems, where they produce novel ideas and ways of thinking about – and seeing – the world, as well as skills and organisational models that other industries can acquire or imitate to enhance their ability to innovate. Some parts of the creative industries, such as digital media, advertising and design, play privileged roles in the innovation system by directly feeding innovation inputs into the production processes of businesses in other sectors. Like technical education and science, the creative industries are viewed as an essential innovative component of a modern post-industrial economy and a primary source of competitive advantage. Change in the creative industries therefore produces structural and not just operational change in the economy. It follows that new opportunities and possibilities will thus emerge from the creative industries for which the economic and welfare effects cannot be known in advance. According to model 4, the creative industries do not drive economic growth directly, as might a boom in the primary resource sector or the housing market, but rather indirectly through the facilitation of the processes of change in the economic order.

The innovation model has emerged only in recent years as an independent rationale for intervention in the creative industries and, as such, is less developed than its market failure, industrial and investment policy counterparts. Its emergence, particularly in Australia (QUT CIRAC and Cutler & Company 2003), the United Kingdom (DCMS, 2008) and, more recently, other parts of Europe (European Commission, 2010), is linked to parallel developments in new growth theory, institutional economics and evolutionary economics, which emphasise the importance of 'intangible' investments (in particular, knowledge) and innovation (which begins with creativity) as long-term sources of productivity growth and competitiveness.

The models historicised

These models have an historical dimension which demonstrates the coevolution of cultural value, regulatory action and the economy in the post-Second World War West. First, the state – at least in the West – developed a role, from around the mid-20th century, to address market failure by asserting the ameliorating and elevating role of the arts (the values expressed in the arts can never, finally, be reconciled with those of the market). The state then engaged in regulation and in support of what came to be dubbed the 'cultural' industries, where popular cultural value was significantly embodied in the products and services of these industries, but they needed protection from the market's levelling of cultural value. Later, the high relative growth in the creative sector led to 'creative industry' development strategies based on the healthiness of traditional macroeconomic indicators (GDP, employment, export growth) and microeconomic indicators (enterprise sustainability) and the beginnings of the mainstreaming of cultural activity in the knowledge-intensive services economy. Finally, the crisis in mass-media business models and the rapid coevolution of the market and household sectors (which we will come to shortly in this chapter) suggest that addressing future potential sources of value creation and the nature and structure of future markets will have much to do with emergent population-wide cultural resources.

Each of these models of the relation of the cultural to the economic overlays rather than overshadows the others. Each has a quite specific account of cultural value. Each stood in a critical relation to the dominant formations of their time and each had a potentially progressive function.

Implications for economics of contemporary dynamics of change

Ballon points to how much media economics will be impacted by technology changes arising from Moore's Law and Metcalfe's Law (2014, pp. 83–87). Moore's Law states that the number of transistors on integrated circuits doubles approximately every two years and has been an accurate description of the logarithmic increase in processing capacity. We see its outworkings in continuously rising technological capabilities, increasing miniaturisation, rapidly falling ICT equipment costs and the diffusion of ICT across many, if not most, economic and social sectors, giving rise to the idea of ICT as a general-purpose technology. This is now driving the notion that 'in the Internet economy the largest economic gains would arise from the production and distribution of digital content... instead of from the commoditized hardware and transmission networks carrying this content' (Ballon, 2014, p. 84).

Ballon argues that professionally produced content has not (because of IPR, falling production costs, consumer reluctance) succeeded in becoming the main engine of economic activity over the Internet. Instead, 'new media companies have to build a business upon the low-cost or even "free" provision of large quantities of easily navigable content and applications that are often produced and/or put online by the end users themselves' (p. 84) and that, despite overstated claims, Moore's Law has 'come to represent the continuing oversupply of new media' (p. 85). Ballon concludes that in this context, 'value shifts even more towards capturing and exploiting the attention of the consumer' (p. 85). We should 'assume that, in an information economy, the real scarce commodity will always be human attention and that attracting that attention will be the necessary precondition of social change. And the real source of wealth' (Lanham, quoted in Ballon, 2014, p. 85).

If Moore's Law leads us towards the idea that Attention is King, Metcalfe's Law suggests that Connectivity is King. Metcalfe's Law states that 'the systemic value of compatibly communicating devices grows as the square of the number'. The value of a communication network rises quadratically with the number of users, while costs rise in a linear fashion. This, as we have seen in Chapter 1, has given rise to the booming sub-discipline of network economics studying network effects.

Metcalfe's Law 'reinforced the general assumption during the height of the internet boom that, once a critical mass of users was reached, these effects would ensure very rapid growth and equally large profits' (Ballon, 2014, p. 86). In hindsight, this was a hazardous prediction. A key indirect network effect is that digital media creates an additional dependency of users of a certain platform upon producers of complementary goods and services – these are called lock-in strategies. And even though entry barriers have been lowered (Moore's Law), concentration worries are far from over – market domination and new media companies have been a recurrent theme in policy debates over the past 20 years. Metcalfe's Law has been criticised as an overstatement of the value of communication networks. Ballon writes that only a part of the total number of connected users may meaningfully interact with each other; the value of a network may decline as information overload/spam come into play, and that affinity between users, rather than simple number of connections, needs to be taken into account. Also, it favours business models that exploit user involvement and interaction by collecting very detailed user data in order to enable more targeted advertising strategies based on the more accurate estimation of individual willingness-to-pay. We revisit this in Chapter 5.

Referring to the previous section, we can regard, in the light of this discussion of the nature of contemporary change, that business, innovation and product cycles are accelerating. Evolutionary economics and its sister approaches, innovation economics and information economics, we suggest, are well equipped to deal with these kinds of transformations.

The kinds and scope of change outlined above suggests that to some degree a fundamental reshaping of media markets is occurring. As we have seen, there are many fine primers on the economics of established media industries. Instead, this chapter is organised around what is happening with media *outside* markets; with *pre-market* media formations; with the relation between *informal* and *formal* media markets; and finally with the notion of *'post-market'* – what happens with media in its post-consumption formation. The inadequacies of measuring what counts as an economy – the 'leading indicators', particularly GDP and GNP, but also inflation, trade figures – have been known for a long time among economists. This has led to such experiments as Bhutan's measures of 'Gross National Happiness' and the Sarkozy Commission's investigation of alternative measures of societal well-being, and economic, environmental and social sustainability. GDP, for example,

does not – and cannot – account for nonmarket leisure activities. It cannot encompass activities that exist beyond the reach of the state, such as the so-called invisible economy of cash transactions, cash remittances from immigrant workers delivered by wire, and the informal trade of services, all of which certainly adds up to many trillions of dollars globally.

(Karabell, 2014, p. 90)

Evolutionary economics, and its resolute focus on the dynamics of change, brings these and other dynamics into sharp focus, and it is this analytical focus on the contingency, variability and historicity of market economies, and on what lies around, before and after the market, that structures our approach in this chapter.

Nature of market capitalism

Before this, however, we must stress that, despite the limits of markets, the need for regulation and the huge range of human activity that occurs outside markets, virtually any recognisable form of economics (orthodox, heterodox and even Communist (see, for example, Li, 2009)) shares a firm regard for the efficiency with which markets distribute knowledge, perform hugely complex coordination functions from the bottom-up and grow wealth. A defining principle underpinning the functioning of modern economies is that markets are – in general – the most efficient mechanism to allocate scarce resources towards the production of goods and services satisfying alternative (and competing) needs. As we saw in Chapter 1, this harks all the way back to Adam Smith's (1991 [1776]) 'Invisible Hand' theorem, according to which the actions of self-interested individuals aggregate into socially desirable outcomes and support a sophisticated division of labour that is conducive to productive efficiency (and therefore wealth creation). And Friedrich Hayek, to whom many heterodox strands of economics are indebted, stresses that markets are much more effective than other alternatives (in particular, central planning as practised under 20th-century Communism) in promoting experimentation and learning to resolve economic problems, harnessing the multifarious pools of knowledge distributed across the economy and society (Hayek, 1945).

Socialist and social democratic political systems and parties understand that well-functioning markets are the bedrock of a healthy social fabric. The Australian social democratic historian, political scientist and economist Hugh Stretton has written:

> wherever markets work as they should, especially where they work without generating undue inequalities of wealth or power, Left thinkers should value them as highly as any privatiser does. Indeed, more highly: the Left as such necessary tasks for government, and so much to lose from inefficient or oppressive bureaucracy, that it should economise bureaucracy every way it can.
>
> (1987, p. 27)

The reason for belabouring this possibly obvious point is that there is a discernible strand of normatively anti-market thinking in our discipline fields. Graeme Turner (2011, p. 688) has defined the politics and ethics of cultural studies as revolving around 'an applied critique of the social and political effects of a market economy' and expressed concern that any more positive appraisal of the role markets play in the allocation of cultural resources would constitute a 'surrender of the politics of Cultural Studies to the interests of the market' (p. 689). But it has actually been a feature of at least some work within media, communication and cultural studies to identify a positive role for markets in acting as complex signalling devices for diverse cultural needs and preferences and providing a stimulus to innovation in the cultural sphere.

In his well-known analysis of cultural policy for the left-wing Greater London Council in the 1980s, Nicholas Garnham argued against 'idealist' traditions in cultural policy that rejected the role played by markets in the allocation of cultural resources, instead observing that 'while this tradition has been rejecting the market, most people's cultural needs and aspirations are being, for better or worse, supplied by the market as goods and services' (1987, p. 25). More recently, Garnham has observed that cultural production under capitalism is not characterised by ideologically driven censorship or insufficient diversity of content, but rather that capitalism has made more cultural product available and 'has clearly widened cultural diversity on both a national and international scale, even if it continues to be unevenly spread' (Garnham, 2011, p. 45). Even a fierce critic of 'market values' and 'cool capitalism' such as Jim McGuigan has observed that 'not even dyed-in-the-wool socialists would today deny the efficacy of a market mechanism in regulating supply and demand, and in setting prices' (McGuigan, 2009, p. 129). So rather than constructing markets as a rhetorical 'bad other' to a prior 'Golden Age' of citizenship, the public good and collective institutions, we argue that media, communications and cultural studies needs to better understand how markets work in contemporary media industries and that the various strands of economic thought we canvas in this book provide valuable resources for undertaking such a task.

Graham Murdock's recent (2013) contribution to fundamental inquiry into the 'historical and normative foundations of communication research' focuses on three 'coexisting moral economies of communicative activity'. The sphere of Capital is a sphere of markets, commodities, consumers and personal possession. The sphere of Government is one of public goods, citizens, shared access and equality.

Table 4.2   Three moral economies

Spheres	Capital	Government	Civil society
Goods	Commodities	Public goods	Gifts
Arenas	Markets	Polities	Networks
Payments	Prices	Taxes	Reciprocities
Relations	Personal possession	Shared access	Co-creation
Identities	Consumers	Citizens	Communards
Ethos	Individual liberty	Equality	Mutuality

Source: Murdock (2013, p. 157). Reproduced under the Creative Commons licence.

The sphere of Civil Society is based on gifts, co-creation and mutuality (Table 4.2).

For Murdock, there is a normative gulf between the 'valorization of consumption and personal possession' (2013, p.157) in the moral economy of Capital and the moral economies of Government and Civil Society. Murdock allows for significant synergy between public goods and gifting (characteristics of Government and Civil Society), but these synergistic moral economies are 'continually compromised by the concerted push toward commercial enclosure' (2013, p. 157). He uses the deep history of the commons of pre-industrial England to illustrate what he regards as a stark zero-sum game: the more markets grew, the more market economics stripped away the 'social and moral context' and 'relegated' principles underpinning the two major forms of non-market economic organisation – public goods and gift relations – and this relegation is ongoing to the present (2013, p. 156).

Murdock uses the term 'public goods' to represent that cluster of public cultural and communications institutions (e.g. libraries, galleries, museums, public service broadcasting) 'founded to address the perceived limits of market-based activity' (2013, p. 157). This is a received and largely unexceptional use of the term 'public goods' (although we nuance it in Chapter 5). But there is an economic understanding of the term – as we shall see in the following section on 'Market or Household' – which underlines the degree to which economies and societies increasingly based on information undermine hard and fast silo-like divisions between markets, households and civil society. We question whether the chasm between Capital, on the one hand, and Government and Civil Society, on the other, accurately captures the way contemporary media economies are structured and experienced. There are other histories, as well, of capitalism that demand our attention.

A similarly deep history of the moral economies attending the explosive growth of wealth attendant on post-Industrial Revolution market capitalism would demonstrate the enduring imbrication of values of self-sacrifice, austerity, good order and social prosperity with participation in the market. Murdock himself starts his article with the reminder that Adam Smith should be regarded as much as the author of *The Theory of Moral Sentiments* as he is of *The Wealth of Nations*. Classic Weberian concerns over the rationalisation and secularisation of the motives behind participation in the market have arisen constantly through the history of Western capitalism. The deeply embedded 'redemptive promise of austerity' attendant on post-global financial crisis economies testifies to the enduringly complex moral economies of Capital (Konings, 2013).

In her deep histories of the rise of capitalism, the polymath Deirdre McCloskey, distinguished professor of Economics, History, English and Communication and adjunct professor of Philosophy and Classics at the University of Illinois at Chicago, insists that:

> A seventeenth change in rhetoric *about* prudence, and about the other virtues exercised in a commercial society, started the material and spiritual progress. Meaning and ethics became for the first time in history favourable to frenetic, unregulated innovation.... I claim here that the modern world was made by a new, faithful dignity accorded to the bourgeois, to take his place, and by a new hopeful liberty, to venture forth. To take one's place and to venture, both the dignity and the liberty, were new, and both were necessary.
>
> (McCloskey, 2013, pp. 8, 10–11)

McCloskey has written a trilogy of books on the 'Bourgeois Era', the explosive growth of wealth in the West occasioned by Industrial Revolution: *The Bourgeois Virtues: Ethics for an Age of Commerce* (2006), *Bourgeois Dignity: Why Economics Can't Explain the Modern World* (2010) and *The Treasured Bourgeoisie: How Markets and Innovation Became Ethical, 1600–1848, and Then Suspect* (Forthcoming). She argues capitalism 'is an ethically drenched human activity' which invokes attention to all of the classical seven virtues.

The tendency in the discipline field to normatively condemn values driving participation in market capitalism needs to be contrasted with the degree to which economics has attempted to grasp intangibles, estimate economic value for nonmarket activities and to 'value' cultural activity in its disciplinary terms. These efforts are well developed but appropriately modest in what they themselves claim. Such efforts can include the development of measures of the value of beauty (Bakhshi, 2010) and of intrinsic value (Bakhshi *et al.*, 2009). They also include concepts such as merit goods (those that society might regard as necessary because of need rather than want and ability to pay); experience goods (the enjoyment of cultural goods and services increases with experience of them), existence value (the value people derive from knowing that something, for example the pristine environment, exists even if it is not directly experienced) and contingent valuation (a method to quantify willingness to pay for a particular environmental good or service; an imputed price to value non-market entities). For example, a contingent valuation of the British Library in 2003 concluded that 'non-use' values, according to the general public, accounted for the majority of the British Library's overall value (Pung *et al.*, 2004).

The point is that notions of critics in media, communication and cultural studies that values of the market – economic values – necessarily debase cultural values and suborn public values reveal less about the interdependencies of economy, culture and society and more about the intellectual boundaries the discipline may have set for itself. It also contrasts with the lengths to which the discipline of economics has attempted to take seriously the predominance of human activity not captured by the market price mechanism (even if at the same time it is fundamentally based on how much *is* captured and made possible by the market price mechanism).

Market or household?

Central to Hugh Stretton's (2000) social democratic vision for economics is his insistence that the 'productive institutions' that constitute an economy include not only private enterprises but equally households and public enterprises (Stretton 2000, pp. 287–328). In economics, there is a long history of work seeking to estimate the economic value produced by the household or non-market sector (see, for example, Hoa and Ironmonger, 2005; Ironmonger 2011, Ironmonger and Soupourmas, 2011). Much heterodox economic thinking has been directed towards re-evaluating the critical role that household labour, particularly women's labour, plays in supporting the market economy. Without such labour – unpaid, and therefore not brought to book in the national accounts – the market economy would collapse, as feminist economics especially has shown.

But the notion of household, outside-market productivity takes on very media-specific importance when we consider the impact of new media affordances and the economics of such affordances. John Quiggin sets the scene:

> The rise of New Media associated with the Internet has radically changed many aspects of daily life, and enabled us to do things that would have seemed unimaginable even a few decades ago. The speed and volume of communications has increased by factor of a million or more since the Internet first emerged in the 1990s, and there has been a corresponding proliferation of information. Yet the economic implications of New Media are hard to discern.
>
> (Quiggin, 2013, p. 90)

Quiggin quotes the famous observation of Nobel prize-winning economist Robert Solow (1987) that 'You can see the computer age everywhere but in the productivity statistics' (2013, p. 90). Our observations about the rapid revenue growth of the major digital platforms, the monetisation of online content and the stabilisation of e-commerce in Chapter 5 will demonstrate that Solow's observation is beginning to show its age. Nevertheless, nothing detracts from the remarkable ways in which digital media and communication has transformed household productivity.

This involves understanding the basics of 'information' economics. Information is perhaps the best example of a public good we have. As we saw in Chapter 1, a public good is one that is non-rivalrous and non-excludable. Non-rivalrous means that if you consume the good, it is still available for others to consume it. Non-excludable means that once it is produced it is not possible to prevent others from consuming it. Quiggin says that information is 'completely nonrival and largely nonexcludable' (2013, p. 91). Without public goods (and public 'bads', such as pollution), it would be difficult to justify much more of a role for government action in the economy apart from its establishment and enforcement of property rights. Of course, the special qualities of media information have been recognised as central issues in both neo-classical and political economics. But the fundamental point about new digital media and communication, and one that justifies the moniker 'revolution'– even from a rigorous debunker of faddish economic thinking such as John Quiggin (see, for example, Quiggin, 2010) – is that it has driven the marginal cost of distributing information almost to zero, increased its volume and quality to an almost unthinkable degree and has made its non-excludability much, much harder (we will take up the subject of piracy in the next section).

On the market side, leading figures in information economics (e.g. Lamberton, 2006) and cultural economics (e.g. Cowen, 2008) have bought into the notion of an information 'revolution' driven to new scale by the Internet. There are now well-established methods for measuring the impact of the information 'revolution' in the market economy. Large claims are made, particularly by those with strategic investment in advice to business. McKinsey (2011), for example, claims that large enterprises have created significant value from dynamic, diversified supply chains, global talent sourcing and analysis of large data sets. But the impact is more profound for SMEs and start-ups. SMEs using web technologies grew more than twice as fast as those with minimal web presence, brought in twice as much revenue through exports as a percentage of sales and created more than twice as many jobs. The Internet has seen the emergence of micro-multinationals that start with operations and business relationships in multiple countries. A similar industry-boosting Deloitte study (Sweney, 2012) on the economic amenity generated by social media looked at the direct economic impact of Facebook – such as paying tax, profits and wages – as well as the more broad impact it has had in enabling businesses to reach customers, make sales, create and monetise apps and even boost demand for products such as broadband and smartphones.

But creative destruction cuts both ways and, demonstrating why Solow's observation remains pertinent, Brynjolfsson and McAfee's (2011) account of *How the Digital Revolution is Accelerating Innovation, Driving Productivity, and Irreversibly Transforming Employment and the Economy* points to the job destruction accompanying digital transformation and the 'jobless recovery' experienced in the United States in the aftermath of the GFC. Not only that, but we are still far away from a time when digitally-based media businesses are as stable, profitable and can offer career stability and progression as those incumbents which they are threatening.

Meanwhile, clear productivity gains, and undoubted increases in welfare, have been occurring at the household level. There is a well-established literature that examines the impact of 'general purpose technologies' (GPTs, which are foundational technologies that affect an entire economy, such as steam, steel, aircraft, microelectronics, ICTs) on economic productivity and growth (see Bresnahan and Trajtenberg, 1995; Lipsey *et al.*, 2005). In the case of digital media and communications, the benefits have been seen first and foremost *outside the market, in the household*. Massive increases in access to information and entertainment, recording, copying, transmission, interaction and participation have occurred in a decade since the advent of Web 2.0/social media. A clear consequence has been steep rises in the costs to households of bandwidth, telecommunications contracts and media devices. Offsetting these costs has been an appreciable recognition by consumers of the uncosted benefits that accrue with Web 2.0/social media engagement and use.

Economists have sought to capture the ostensible value of these off-market affordances. One such methodology is based on the notion of 'consumer surplus'. Consumer surplus is the value of the benefit consumers derive by being able to consume a product or service for a price lower than the most that they would be willing to pay. Brynjolfsson, Hu and Smith (2003), for example, found that it was possible to quantify the enhanced consumer welfare of increased product variety in online bookstores contrasted with the consumer welfare gain from increased competition and lower prices in the book market. They found it to be between 7 and 10 times the size of lower prices – a precise exemplification of Metcalfe's Law. Boston Consulting Group (Belza *et al.*, 2012, p. 5) has claimed that in Australia:

- Internet media content is delivering a consumer surplus – the value that consumers place on an activity or a product that is over and above the price they pay for it – of AU$24 billion in year;
- Of this, the largest single contribution comes from online content portals. Consumers pay nothing directly, but they deliver a nationwide benefit valued at more than AU$9 billion per year;
- Online platforms play a key enabling role in delivering choice and providing opportunities for creators and produces to reach local, national and global audiences;
- Australians believe the media landscape is improving, with more good-quality content available both online and offline;
- Australia has a trade surplus in online video, exporting more than it imports. Twice as much Australian online video is consumed in the United States than is consumed in Australia. ('Trade surplus' is a very tendentious term, as a vast majority of this content is not traded but circulated free.)

The formal–informal market interface

An evolutionary perspective will also focus not only on that which occurs outside of markets but also on the borderlands between types of markets. Neoclassical approaches will tend to focus on and seek to substantiate or refute claims for larger or smaller impacts on the market economy from piracy and other informal media activity. On the other hand, a good deal of political economy, based on its tendency to adopt anti-corporate, anti-big business stances, may adopt 'copyleft' positions. In contrast, evolutionary approaches will tend to focus on the wider ecology: how informal activity reshapes markets, continuities between licit and illicit informality, the interdependence of the informal and formal and the potential for innovation arising from informal activity.

The informal economy is that wide range of activity that is not registered in official national accounts. It exists on a continuum from licit (e.g. secondary markets such as second-hand books) to contingently illicit (e.g. irregular bedroom downloading) to industrial-scale piracy. Informal economies are significant in size and globally pervasive. Austrian economist Friedrich Schneider, known for his international estimates of informal economic activity, puts the figure at an average of 37% of GDP for sub-Saharan Africa and Central Asia, and an average of 13% in OECD countries (Schneider *et al.*, 2010). According to Ramon Lobato and Julian Thomas (2015), while international debates on piracy would suggest a fundamental tension between the informal and formal media economy, there is, and always has been, a dynamic, constantly evolving, interplay between processes of formalisation and informalisation.

Lobato and Thomas offer the BBC as an example of this interplay, arguing that while the BBC is the quintessential formal media organization – 'a model public enterprise, born during a time – the interwar years – of institutional experimentation and increasing state involvement in the economy' (2015, p. 37) – it, like most media organizations, 'is engaged in a series of complex interactions with the informal realm' that occur 'right across the organization's extraordinary array of production, distribution and market activities' (2015, p. 37). These include the BBC's extensive work with amateur and user-generated content, its open access BBC Creative Archive, its employment of talent whose skills have been honed in informal settings and its development of the Internet-based catch-up service iPlayer – a mechanism Lobato and Thomas see as 'formalizing the hitherto informal practices of personal recording and playback' (2015, p. 38).

This, also, has got to do with the nature of (formal) media as information goods. While the cost of producing the first copy may require substantial investment, subsequent copies are relatively cheap to make. In other words, the 'marginal costs' of producing additional units are relatively low. This distinctive production cost structure creates both opportunities and challenges. On the one hand, success in the market can generate substantial benefits because the low marginal cost structure enables production to be scaled up quickly and at little cost. On the other hand, there is a greater likelihood of 'cannibalisation' of sales through piracy (legal and illegal copies become closer substitutes in the eyes of consumers when the differences in quality between them are small and the costs of copying are low). This has implications for policy – the prospect of high and rapid economic returns on public investment should make new media a ripe target for industrial policy-makers, while the challenge of piracy also warrants the attention of policy-makers, even if there is little agreement on what measures are needed to address it.

This is not only because there is substantial 'consumer surplus' that arises from informal uses of media but also because of the inextricable interrelationships of the formal and the informal. Lobato and Thomas show enduring informal practices within formal systems that include the following:

- gap filling (consumers sharing infrastructure such as satellite dishes, or network employees adjusting their work schedules to see project deadlines);
- incubating (skills and ideas developed in informal contexts are taken up by informal industries);
- outsourcing (formal sector acquires services or skills from the informal environment because it is more efficient and flexible to do so);
- taste-testing (companies like Netflix monitoring heavily downloaded shows as a way of estimating the market for the future productions);
- priming (using informal practices to promote demand informal markets); and
- educating (informal services are sometimes the first places where businesses and consumers acquaint themselves with emerging technologies, services or products).

(Lobato and Thomas, 2015, p. 31)

And they also show the effects of informal activity on formal markets are pervasive:

- substitution (where activities associated with one market zone are transferred to the other, such as when a new technology or medium

emerges to provide a comparable service – an example being the toppling of Encyclopaedia Britannica by Wikipedia);
- dispersal (where market activities diverge and economic transactions become more diffuse, an example being the noted increase in 'cable cutting' that has shadowed increases in home Internet expenditures)
- extension (where informal markets increase demand in formal sectors, such as the formation of new advertising markets around user-generated content);
- revaluation (the impact of informal markets changes formal market value; for example, brand dilution associated with counterfeiting);
- redeployment (technologies and methods developed in one market are repurposed in the other, such as the formalisation of peer-to-peer networking through applications like Skype);
- reconfiguration (where activity in one market forces change in the organisational logics of the other; for example, a reduction in unit pricing in order to compete with pirating practices).

(Lobato and Thomas, 2015, p. 32–6)

It is important in critical accounts of media economics not to normatively overvalue the informal, particularly when dealing with those economies where there is more than sufficient capacity to pay for media goods and services. And in relation to developing economies, we also need to be careful not to idealise the informal economy, as it frequently involves the exploitation of the vulnerable and the undermining of more collective solutions that engage the local creative producers themselves. The formal–informal innovation dynamic also spills over into debates about closed and open systems. It is often assumed in these debates that 'openness' (the mutuality and collective informal action displayed in the open source software movement, business models based on open innovation (Cheeseborough, 2006; Von Hippel, 2006) is a better model than proprietary enclosures of intellectual property.

But take the case of Apple. While the iPhone might be considered a throwback when compared to the open architecture of the PC and Android systems (Zittrain, 2008), Apple's iTunes and App Store were the first to solve the micropayment issue, thus providing a secure environment for e-commerce in media entertainment space, as well as sparking a wave of innovation that brought about a gradual restructuring of the mobile value chain – as new kinds of locational, educational, social, entertainment and gaming software were introduced – and a shift in value from the traditional pillars of the mobile economy (telecommunications services, mobile handsets) to a rapidly growing 'mobile app economy' that also includes in-app purchases and in-app advertising.

But having said that, it is important to offer the other, very contemporary side of the coin: informalisation as a business model. One of television's biggest global hits of 2012–4 was *Game of Thrones*, a fantasy drama produced by the US cable network Home Box Office (HBO). The series was a broadcast hit, and the box sets and digital downloads broke records for HBO. TorrentFreak also named it the most pirated show in 2012 and 2013. Officials from HBO have acknowledged that piracy around the show has created a 'cultural buzz'. When discussing the issue of piracy, Jeff Bewkes, chief executive of Time Warner, HBO's parent company, claimed that

> we've been dealing with this issue for years with HBO…people have always been running wires down on the back of apartment buildings and sharing with their neighbours. Our experience is, it all leads to more penetration, more paying subs, more health for HBO, less reliance on having to do paid advertising…*Game of Thrones* is the most pirated show in the world. Well, you know, that's better than an Emmy!

> (Hickey, 2013)

Piracy

As noted above, piracy is a landmine for policy-makers and industry while forming a substantial component of the headily titled 'consumer surplus' generated by digital affordances. Piracy attracts a bewildering array of claims and counterclaims. Industry sources make eye-watering claims about the costs of piracy while economists can be sharply divided on its deficits and benefits. One estimate found that piracy cost the Motion Pictures Association of America (MPAA) studios $6.1 billion in lost revenue in 2005, with a comprehensive estimate of losses closer to $20.5 billion annually (including broader and associated industry earnings, absence of job creation and lost tax revenue) (Siwek, 2006). And historian of piracy Adrian Johns (2012), references a figure as high as $1 trillion lost through both piracy and counterfeiting. Ronald Bettig (1996) thinks piracy is resistance to capitalist exploitation while Stephen Siwek (2006) is a major advocate for the industry's concerns. And there is very much a 'moral economy' attending its practices, hedged on all sides by the socio-economic

(Continued)

circumstances in which it occurs. Apropos 'consumer surplus', an economically literate blogger comments that 'the treatment of some piracy as "economically optimal" is disconcerting to those (of us) who actually pay for everything ... obscuring certain moral principles by speaking about it only in the form of consumer surplus' (Rao, 2013). And just as multifarious are the responses which have been enjoined by and on industry and policy makers. As well as the obvious option of stricter enforcement of intellectual property rights, other approaches include digital rights management solutions, the compensation of rights holders through levies on technologies that can be used to make illegal copies (though there are good economic reasons for avoiding this) or measures to lower the transaction costs of copyright licensing to enable the development of new business models (Hargreaves, 2011).

Piracy evokes such varying perspectives because it is a dynamic, evolving phenomenon. Ramon Lobato (2012), in his account of informal film distribution, breaks the phenomenon down from six perspectives: piracy as theft, free enterprise, free speech, authorship, resistance and as access. In what follows, we are indebted to Lobato's critical reading of copyright infringement (2012, pp. 72–85).

1. *Theft:* piracy as theft is the dominant discourse, at least in high-income countries with capacity to pay, and those with copyright industry export capacity. This is embedded in US policy, which has been the key driver of international intellectual property maximalism, and is exemplified by the MPAA's 'war on piracy [which] strives to embed an ethics of copyright in the global mindset' (Lobato, 2012, p. 71). Counterintuitively, the United States' IP maximalism in seeking to protect its major export industry sits alongside its fair use doctrines which allow a greater degree of discretion in the use of copyrighted material for a range of basically non-commercial purposes than in many other countries. Industry claims of the losses due to piracy have been questioned on the basis that they have often been based on the dubious assumption that for each movie accessed illegally, a legitimate version of the same film went unsold. And such figures have been bolstered by using gross rather than net figures which are necessarily suspect

(Continued)

because, by definition, piracy operates 'off the books' and cannot be accurately accounted for.

2. *Free enterprise*: there is a strong strand in economic thought which can read piracy as the purest form of free enterprise. Bettig (1996) argues that greater efficiency would result in a radically liberalised regulatory environment where reduction in returns to copyright holders would be offset by productivity gains arising from lower prices and wider availability of cultural goods. This argument for 'weak copyright' is based on the notion of piracy as a 'business force' (Johns, 2010) – the notion that while copyright protects one kind of economic activity, in doing so it stifles the possibility of other, perhaps more creative, revenue-generating arrangements. This idea links with the notion of piracy as driving innovation. For example, the threat of piracy has driven Hollywood to experiment with changes to release windowing and a much greater use of day-and-date (simultaneous release in several territories). It can even lead to an acceptance within the industry, as we saw with HBO and *Game of Thrones*, that piracy is the 'first window' that can be used to actually bolster legal consumption and create cultural buzz around a product.

3. *Free speech*: Lobato (2012, p.76) argues that some of the most effective critiques of current copyright regimes have come from the bosom of the 'Californian ideology' – tech-savvy American liberals espousing quintessential American values of informational freedom and personal liberty. This position has given rise to Creative Commons, an easy-to-use alternative to standard copyright licensing which has enhanced amateur, not-for-profit re-use and remixing as well as revolutionised access to official documentation for citizens and business use.

4. *Authorship*: this approach concerns the 'deconstruction' of the notion of authorship as such, questioning the notion of 'creation' of works. Given that all so-called creation is recombination, difference between authorship and piracy is only a matter of degree rather than of kind.

5. *Resistance*: certain strands of radical political economy espouse a notion of piracy as resistance, treating copyright regimes as hegemonic legal institutions which convert information and

---

(Continued)

labour into capital. Bettig's authoritative *Copywriting Culture: The Political Economy of Intellectual Property* subscribes to this approach. Pang (2006) argues that, because Hollywood has freely pilfered textual content from Asian cinemas while simultaneously waging rhetorical war against copyright infringement, piracy can be viewed 'as a critical interrogation of today's international cultural politics' (2006, p. 82).

6. *Access*: while most debate about piracy is conducted around Western assumptions, this approach focuses on the practices of everyday piracy taking place in low-income, developing country contexts where accessing media legally is not an option. It reinforces Joe Karaganis' (2011) point that, seen in a global perspective, piracy is less an ethical than a pricing issue. Ravi Sundaram's *Pirate Modernity: Delhi's Media Urbanism* (2009), a thick description of everyday, street level, non-legal Indian media practices, exemplifies this approach.

Coevolution and 'social network markets'

A particularly relevant feature of the dynamics of media formalisation and informalisation can be understood as 'coevolution' and gives rise to what has been dubbed 'social network markets'. This is the idea that there is a coevolutionary dynamic building between the world of social media and the market economies of formal media. Coevolution 'occurs when another species, technology or market is the reciprocal selection environment' (Hartley *et al.*, 2013, p. 98). In this case, social media and the major new digital platforms on which social media activity is performed are becoming increasingly the 'selection environment' within which new innovative forms of screen content and screen distribution strategy – indeed, we might say the future of screen industries – are being shaped. Substantial slices of previously amateur social media, reciprocally, are being shaped by their encounter with the market. This has been called the *monetisation* of amateur media and the *socialisation* of professional media (see Cunningham, 2012, 2013).

Brian Arthur is a leading evolutionary theorist of technology and provides the broader context for this media-specific process. His *The Nature of Technology: What it is and How it Evolves* (2009) describes the potentially profound economic change which can occur when society encounters a new body of technology: 'The economy reacts to the new body's presence, and in doing so changes its activities, its industries, its organisational arrangements – its structures. And if the resulting change in the economy is important enough we call that a revolution (2009, p. 146). The social domain and the economy 'mutually co-adapt and mutually create the new' (2009, p. 155).

Social network markets (Potts *et al.*, 2008) is a concept developed to account for ways in which formal market-based activity and informal social or household activity are converging as a distinctive feature of the contemporary, especially digitally enabled, economy. A social network market is one where individual consumer choices are determined by the choices of others. The concept describes the nature of consumer choice and producer decision-making under conditions where price signals are not prime or sufficient information, and where therefore one's choice is based on others' choices due to uncertainties about product quality arising from novelty or complexity, or the cost of acquiring this information oneself. We have already seen, in the Introduction, that prices in media markets can be less efficient carriers of all necessary information about supply and demand, including the product's production costs, characteristics, consumer preferences and willingness to pay. Social network markets compensate for this, and often describe the crucible of new or emergent markets that, typically, arise from non-market dynamics (e.g. digital and Internet affordances) and that often stay at the complex borderland between social networks and established markets.

This describes the recent history and new ecology of US television very well, a media environment in which 'fanbases' rather than 'audiences' are what makes for success. In the words of Alex Carloss (quoted in Dredge, 2014), YouTube's global head of entertainment, 'an audience tunes in when they're told to, a fanbase chooses when and what to watch. An audience changes the channel when the show is over. A fan base shares, it comments, it generates, it creates'. An extended study of this illustrative case is provided in Chapter 5.

Conclusion

This chapter has provided an overview of the contribution evolutionary economics might make to analysing issues central to media, communication and cultural studies. It needed, first, to tackle foundational issues grounding the reluctance, in the humanities, to assess the relevance of the evolutionary paradigm. We argue that evolutionary economics provides a non-teleological, non-totalistic account of the dynamics of capitalism that is as dynamically conflictual as its Marxist counterpart and can provide us with a theoretical and historical framework for a more adequate understanding of the nature, scope and rate of change media industries are undergoing, and the effects of media in society. We have pursued this by concentrating on the theme of the evolving nature of markets and the shifting borderlands between markets and non-market household and social activity. The phenomena central to these contemporary relationships – social media, digital convergence, media user agency, including such 'landmine' matters as piracy and new concepts like 'social network markets' – are, or should be, the speciality of media, communication and cultural studies. This makes the lessons we might draw from evolutionary economics for disciplinary advancement a 'natural' fit.

There are other angles on the dynamics of change and their implications for media markets. Taking one important example, if it was the case that a sixth Kondratieff–Schumpeter wave is occurring, a wave 'in which economic growth is no longer dependent on the irreversible consumption of resources' (Moody and Nogrady, 2010), then there would need to be solutions to the 'post-consumption' life of media hardware. An important literature in environmental economics and media studies has drawn needed attention to the markets for the disposal of relatively highly toxic media hardware (Pellow and Park, 2002; Smith *et al.*, 2006; Grossman, 2007; Maxwell and Miller, 2012; Gabrys, 2013; see also the journal *Explorations in Media Ecology*), to the planned obsolescence of much contemporary 'smart' technology and to the *diseconomies of scale* of digital platforms (the marginal cost of distribution does not decline, but remains constant as the user base and the demands for bandwidth expand enormously). Future innovations in dealing with such unsustainable features of the contemporary media economy will do much to drive coevolution of social and physical technologies, business strategy and institutional response, further transforming the media economy.

5 Case Studies and Conclusion

After having canvassed traditional neoclassical economics and political economy as the two dominant frameworks, then surveying two alternative economics frameworks, institutional economics and evolutionary economics, we turn in this final chapter to more extended cases that illustrate the ways in which these alternatives sit as explanatory approaches compared to the established approaches.

Public service media

The relevance of different theoretical frameworks discussed in this book can be illustrated with reference to debates about the role and performance of PSBs, or, as they are increasingly being termed in an era of multiplatform media and convergence, PSM – as they are increasingly expected to provide content for diverse publics across multiple platforms (Flew, 2011b). In this section, we will explore approaches from neoclassical media economics and critical political economy, while also identifying insights from NIE and evolutionary economics that can be applied to PSM. The intention is to go beyond familiar arguments for and against publicly funded media. NIE provides analytical tools that identify issues with PSM, such as the challenges of organisational complexity, the complex governance structures of PSM organisations and how best to ensure that their decisions are in the public interest. Some of these issues are similar to those facing commercial media organisations, while others arise from public funding and the public service remit. A case can be made for the continuing importance of PSM in a convergent media environment through evolutionary economics, as it identifies such organisations as important sites of new media innovation with a policy remit and governance framework that enables them to undertake R&D in the public interest that is demonstrably different to the priorities of commercial media corporations. There will be a discussion of the concept of public value tests (PVT) as one means that has been deployed by various governments to benchmark PSM performance in the European context, and the challenges that PVT present in determining the appropriate scope of online activities of PSMs in particular, and their contribution to media system innovation.

Neoclassical economics and PSBs: Market failure

The mainstream economic case for PSB has revolved around the concept of market failure, with particular reference to public goods, externalities and merit goods. As the concept of market failure was discussed in Chapter 1, we will not reiterate all details here. What can be noted is that broadcasting has been seen as being prone to market failure, since spectrum scarcity can set limits to overall channel numbers, although authors such as Coase (1966) contested the 'spectrum scarcity' argument. Perhaps more importantly, over-the-air broadcasting has the characteristics of a public good, in that it is non-excludable (freely available to everyone who owns necessary reception equipment) and non-exhaustible (there are zero marginal costs involved in providing the service to one additional viewer). Broadcasting thus has public goods attributes comparable to national defence, emergency services, lighthouses and basic research, and in all of these areas public provision of such services has been deemed appropriate (Hoskins *et al.*, 2004, pp. 297–99). Moreover, PSBs have been considered a suitable means of generating programming that has merit good attributes (quality programming, programming of national political or cultural significance, programmes aimed at minority communities or interests, educational programming), as they are not beholden to shareholders to make a profit, or obligated to maximise advertiser revenues or audience share across the programming schedule.

The question of how significant market failure arguments for PSB are in an era of digital technologies and multichannel broadcasting remains a subject of contention. Armstrong (2005) has argued that digital subscription broadcasting has significantly weakened market failure rationales for PSB by enabling a wider range of niche channels to be available in fields such as the arts, history or science and allowing the consumer to more directly determine the menu of programme choices available to them. It is also the case that quality television can no longer be deemed to exclusively come from PSBs, if indeed it ever could. In the United States, which remains by far the world's largest television market, the turn to high-concept, edgy and innovative dramas was led by the premium cable network HBO, with shows such as *The Sopranos, The*

Wire, Game of Thrones and *True Detective*, followed by other cable networks such as AMC with *Mad Men* and *Breaking Bad*. Such programmes are big-budget, high-concept TV that is nonetheless premised upon the idea that they will not necessarily appeal to a mass audience, not least because they typically include content that faces restrictions from being broadcast in prime-time programme schedules.

In responding to the challenges of content proliferation and quality niche programming, authors such as Davies (2004) have argued that niche services are not universally available, raising questions of equitable access to public goods. Davies also argued that there continued to be deficiencies in the supply of informational or educative content that may have merit good attributes, even in a multichannel environment. Religious programming is a case in point. Cable services are often awash with channels of various faith-based groups, and there could be little complaint about a lack of access to religious content. But the PSB remit in this area is quite different. It is not to provide content to believers in various religious faiths, but rather to critically reflect on religion and its role in society and enable greater lay understanding of various religious faiths and their relationship to one another in a non-sectarian manner, rather than to promote any particular faith, church or denomination. In that respect, then, there continues to be a 'market failure' in religious programming that arguably only PSBs can adequately address.

At the same time, ubiquitous access to the Internet further complicates the market failure arguments for PSB. For example, if one case for PSB was its ability to cater for cultural and linguistic minorities, it is apparent that such groups can now have good access to content in their own language, or from their homeland communities. Similar points could be made about news and information content, or almost any particular media content area. Media convergence also raises new questions about the involvement of PSBs in the digital environment, or the transition from public service broadcasting to multi-platform PSM. In what ways do the charters of PSBs need to be modified in this new environment? What does the case for market failure look like if one removes the prior rationale of spectrum scarcity as a barrier to entry for new players?

A different problem with the market failure argument for PSB is that very few PSBs were originally created to meet gaps in the menu of commercial broadcast media offerings. Lord Reith's original vision of the BBC had far more to do with the cultural and civilisational missions and the nation-building role of the broadcast medium than with economic concerns, and it is not until the 1980s, when the Thatcher government commissioned the Peacock Committee Review of BBC Financing, that economics became central to debates about the structure of British media. Such concerns were notably absent from earlier public inquiries such as the 1962 Pilkington Report, for instance, and were at the margins of the 1977 Annan Committee Review (Goodwin, 1998). In other countries, we find the path-dependent evolution of public broadcasting driven by questions of bilingualism and multilingualism (e.g. Canada, Belgium), multiculturalism (e.g. Singapore, Malaysia, Australia) and political pluralism (e.g. the Netherlands). Arguably the one country where PSB was established to compensate for perceived gaps in commercial offerings has been the United States, where the Public Broadcasting Service (PBS) has largely functioned since the late 1960s as a niche broadcaster, and as 'a space for the liberal and/or highly educated constituencies... to escape to' (Ouellette and Lewis, 2004, p. 62).

What we find, then, is that debates about whether PSM is warranted on the basis of market failure draw attention to the degree to which neoclassical economics presents us with models decontextualised from questions of culture and history. PSBs have evolved worldwide in a variety of ways, and the path-dependent evolution of such institutions in national media systems is poorly explained by using the blanket 'market failure' rationales. While market failure provides one normative basis for making claims about PSBs in general, it has significant weaknesses in providing a basis for evaluating the structure, conduct and performance of PSBs in practice.

Critical political economy and PSBs: Media citizenship

The approach of critical political economists towards PSBs has varied over time. Early accounts such as those of the Glasgow University Media Group (1976) and leading British media and cultural studies theorists such as Schlesinger (1979), Hall (1986) and Sparks (1986) developed a class-based critique of what they saw as an elitist bias in broadcasters such as the BBC, as well as a propensity to construct a unified national identity in ways that downplayed social divisions based upon class. In more recent work, however, this critical and class-based perspective has been displaced by a more normative account that presents PSBs as being central to nation-building and to furthering the values of citizenship against the commoditised products of the commercial market. Garnham (1990) argued that PSBs were the most significant institutional manifestation of philosopher Jürgen Habermas's normative ideal of a public sphere, dealing with the individual 'as a citizen exercising public rights of debate', rather than as consumers 'within a privatised domestic sphere' (Garnham, 1990, pp. 110–11). Tracey (1998) argued that PSBs were central to an audience-as-citizen model of the media, and that policy-makers had a moral obligation to support PSB as being central to a '"cultural" or "civic" model for the development of broadcasting' (Tracey, 1998, p. 11). Murdock (2013) has argued that public media in all of its forms are rooted in a 'moral economy' of the collective public good, inherently aligned with other public cultural institutions such as public libraries, parks, museums and galleries as part of the rich fabric and entitlements of democratic citizenship and resources for enhancing the quality of communal life.

In considering these arguments for PSM, an issue that arises is what constitutes a PSB, as this is less straightforward than it first appears. Non-commercialism is a difficult distinction to sustain, partly because many PSBs worldwide – possibly the majority – carry commercial advertising. There are also elements of similarity in the incentive structures that exist within PSBs and commercial media, as we will discuss further below. Public ownership is also not in itself a sufficient criterion for PSB status. The world's largest publicly owned broadcaster is now China Central Television (CCTV), yet consideration of the structure and operations of CCTV has thus far been conspicuously absent from most accounts of the future of PSBs. Even those PSBs that do not carry commercial advertising such as the BBC or Australia's ABC are nonetheless engaged in various commercial transactions, including overseas programme sales, selling publications, running shops and online product sales, whose viability is assessed on the basis of their ability to generate new revenues for the organisation.

The definition of PBSs, then, has been as much normative as it has been institutional, constructed around their relationship to discourses of citizenship and the public sphere. What we find, then, is a gap between the normative dimension of PSBs and what they do in practice, or what Collins (2004) referred to as the divide between the 'ises' and the 'oughts' of PSB. PSBs clearly provide a range of popular programmes, whose appeal is measured by the same indicators as those used by commercial media, such as ratings and other audience measurement techniques. This is a manifestation of the practical tension between PSB charters which give them a particular role in providing quality programming and 'leading ... public and popular taste', and the political reality that 'their social productivity (and institutional legitimacy) depends on the degree to which their programs and services are used and valued by listeners and viewers' (Collins, 2004, p. 38).

It has also been noted that features commonly identified as being central to the public service mission – quality and innovative programmes, providing a public space of information and debate, catering to national identity and community, catering for minority tastes and interests – are also provided by commercial media (Jacka, 2003). In Britain, for example, the commercial ITV network is regarded as a PSB even though it is privately owned. ITV has been responsible for pioneering TV programmes in the United Kingdom over many decades as well as those associated with uniquely British attributes of 'quality'; to take a recent example, many outside of Britain are surprised to find that *Downton Abbey* is an ITV programme, since it seems to be a quintessential BBC period drama. We noted earlier that premium cable services such as HBO are clearly involved in the production of quality drama, and it is also notable that 24-hour news services are provided by both PSBs and by commercial providers through dedicated subscription channels. With the development of online services such as Google Books, it is also apparent that a private provider can also achieve a public good such as broadening access to a diverse array of information sources, as noted by US District Court Judge Denny Chin in his 2013 judgement on the *Authors Guild v. Google* case (*Authors Guild v. Google Inc.*, 2013).

New institutional economics and PSM

The accounts of PSM developed in neoclassical economics and critical political economy have different normative bases, with one deriving its arguments from market failure rationales and the other from discourses of citizenship and the public sphere. Both emphasise the degree to which PSM organisations are profoundly different from commercial media; the problem we have identified is whether in practice such a claim is overstated. NIE provides us with different insights into how and why PSM organisations possess similarities to their counterparts in the commercial sector, as well as identifying particular governance challenges in ensuring their responsiveness both to their charter obligations and to the publics they serve.

This should not be read as a critique of PSM in general, nor is it linked to claims that PSMs possess a left-wing political bias. Rather, it is to suggest that there are similar structural challenges in both types of media organisation, such as maximising audience reach, evaluating performance and developing incentive structures. These in turn can lead to similar problems, such as a tendency to over-expand, an accrual of managerial powers that lack adequate oversight and accountability and forms of moral hazard arising from such institutions largely being responsible for regulating their own conduct. Advancing understanding of such issues is unlikely to be helped by simple binary oppositions between 'good' PSM and 'bad' commercial media. We have argued that both the neoclassical media economics approach, based on market failure, and the critical political economy perspective, based around citizenship and the public sphere, remain overly normative in providing frameworks for evaluating the performance of PSM institutions. As both types of organisation increasingly co-exist within a far more complex ecology of convergent media, we believe there is a need to develop more practical and applied understandings of how PSM can flourish and better serve the public good in changing institutional environments. As discussed in Chapter 3, core propositions of NIE are as follows:

1. Firms in both the public and private sectors can be understood as a 'nexus of contracts' and as an institutional form designed to internalise transaction costs in order to better manage complexity in the context of limited (bounded) rationality;
2. Large firms in both the public and private sectors have to deal with the separation of asset ownership from everyday management, and resulting principal-agent problems. In particular, an endemic risk is that of managers acting in ways that maximise their own returns – performance bonuses, higher salaries, more personal status and influence and so on – rather than those of the assets' 'owners' (shareholders, governments or taxpayers);
3. One way in which organisations internalise transaction costs is through vertical integration and conglomeration. This reduces market uncertainty and bargaining costs, but runs the risk of making such organisations more difficult to manage, hosting hostile and conflicting corporate cultures, and becoming increasingly bureaucratic in their operations;
4. Relational contracts, or incentive-based contracts, are an important feature of large firms, as successful performance of work tasks is seen as less dependent on formal management than it is on the talents and motivation of particular individuals, or what is referred to as asset specificity.

As we observed in Chapter 3, all of these issues can be seen to arise in the media industries, where large public and private sector organisations deal with complex production processes, time-dependent media/creative products and endemic uncertainty of demand (Caves,

2000). We can also observe considerable movement of personnel between the public and private sectors, particularly since the 1980s as the pressure for PSM to become more corporatised entities has also seen greater recruitment of managers from the commercial media sector. There are strong commonalities of view among public and private sector media mangers around the desirability of corporate expansion, driven in part by the value attached to economies of scale and scope, the need to maximise market reach and audience share, the perceived power of media brands and, more recently, by the perceived need to be operating across multiple platforms in an era of digital convergence.

There are also considerable commonalities in internal governance structures, particularly as incentive-based contracts for 'star' talent have replaced public service conditions of employment across PSM organisations. In Australia, there was much controversy when the salaries of on-air presenters at the Australian Broadcasting Corporation (ABC) were leaked, showing that some on-air TV and radio presenters were receiving 2–3 times the salaries of others. Perhaps no less significantly, the issue raised here was not only that of whether the public knew how much various news and current affairs hosts were being paid, but the lack of awareness among the staff of how much others were being paid. It thus becomes more difficult than it first appears to distinguish public service and commercial media, as both seek to maximise user reach or audience share, many PSM organisations carry commercial advertising and incentive-based contracts are a feature of both commercial and non-commercial media.

A continuing point of difference between public and private media organisations concerns their ownership and means of accountability. In the case of companies that are privately owned and publicly listed on the share market, evidence of management under-performance can lead to a fall in the share market price, a hostile takeover bid or other forms of action by the owners of the company in response to its management, which may include replacing the management team (Jensen and Meckling, 1976). At least in theory, then, financial markets are meant to provide one countervailing source of power to that of management power.

The equivalent countervailing power for PSMs is that of governments which are the notional 'owners' of PSM assets. But if they were to consider acting to deal with poorly performing management, they would have to deal with the major problem that such actions would invariably be seen as being politically motivated, not least because those subject to such decisions have strong incentives to portray themselves as political victims. Moreover, as PSM have a mix of primarily non-commercial charter-based objectives and market-based measures such as audience share, benchmarking what is adequate performance for such an entity can be difficult to determine. The issue of governance structures that can keep a check on the expansionary ambitions of PSM managers is an issue that is raised even among those supportive of the public service remit. Goodwin (2014) has argued that 'the friends of PSM . . . must adopt a more critical tone in addressing existing PSB operations', citing such problems within PSM organisations as 'bloated executive salaries, conservative programming policies, corporate arrogance, and lack of inclusiveness – to name but four in a list that is not short' (Goodwin, 2014, p. 84).

In attempting to devise a framework that can allow governments as the principal funders of PSM to address principal-agent problems and set limits to managerial autonomy, a difficulty arises in the insistence that PSM organisations must not be subject to forms of government interference or to forms of external regulation that other media entities are subject to. For example, regulation of the BBC by Ofcom is considered to be inappropriate, as the editorial independence and institutional autonomy of the BBC is guaranteed by its Charter, and its accountability must be to the parliament in terms that relate to its underlying legislation, and not to the government of the day. While this guarantee of independence is important in its own right, one consequence is that PSM organisations can be seen to be effectively regulating themselves, which generates considerable moral hazard risks, as those responsible for overseeing the organisation's content remain connected to the organisation.

At the same time, it is important to recognise that ownership and governance structures interact with organisational cultures (Clegg *et al.*, 2005, pp. 267–74). Organisational cultures express themselves most visibly in the artefacts they physically produce and display, which in this instance is most obviously the media content they produce and distribute. But there are also deeper levels of organisational culture that include the values of an organisation, the norms and beliefs of its employees and the 'basic assumptions that shape organisational members' worldviews, beliefs, and norms, which guide their behaviour without being explicitly addressed' (Clegg *et al.*, 2005, p. 272). The distinctiveness of PSM in terms of its history, culture and values becomes particularly important in this regard, as it suggests that a public service orientation may be embedded within the organisational culture. Claims about organisational cultures are notoriously difficult to measure empirically (Clegg *et al.*, 2005, pp. 274–78), but may themselves be factors that promote – or inhibit – innovation within PSM organisations. The sense that control over public institutions has become bound up with the electoral struggle, or what Furubotn and Richter (2005, p. 483) refer to as a 'struggle for political property rights' that in turn shapes public institutions, has heightened concerns within PSM organisations and among their supporters that any changes to existing guarantees of statutory independence would promote direct political interference in decision-making within the organisation.

Evolutionary/innovation economics put to the 'Public Value' test

One way in which governments have sought in recent years to assess the contribution of PSM organisations has been through the application of public value tests to the development of new services (Benington and Moore, 2011). Such tests proposed an operational understanding of public value, whereby strategies could be assessed in terms of: (1) their contribution to outcomes deemed valuable by the community and the government as their elected representatives; (2) their sustainability in terms of gaining ongoing support from key political and other stakeholders; and (3) their feasibility in terms of the funding, technology, staff skills and organisational capabilities needed to deliver the required public value outcomes. The concept emerged in the context of pressures to 'reinvent government' (Osborne and Gaebler, 1992) and largely 'accepted the idea that there was much to be learned from the private sector about how to manage large production organisations successfully' (Benington and Moore, 2011, p. 9).

The BBC adopted the concept of public value with its 'Building Public Value' report, released in 2004 in advance of its Charter renewal in 2005 (Davies, 2004). It argued that 'public value should be the goal for everything that the BBC does' (quoted in Lee *et al.*, 2011, p. 292) and began to apply public value tests to the introduction of new digital services from 2007 (Brevini, 2013, pp. 76–77). The concept of public value came to be increasingly important in Europe over the 2000s, as the result of European Commission policies that gave quite different interpretations to public service broadcasting and online extensions of the public service remit.

The Commission has identified PSB as central to European media pluralism and that its contribution needs to be safeguarded in the Member States of the European Community. This is due to its important role in promoting cultural and linguistic diversity, educational programming, objectively informing public opinion and promoting pluralism and supplying quality programming on a free-to-air basis (Karppinen, 2013, p. 158). At the same time, in the 2009 Communication on State Aid, it took a strong view that extension of PSB activity into the online environment was only warranted where a demonstrable market failure case existed, and where the new service clearly 'added value' in relation to the 'democratic, social and cultural needs' deemed central to the public service remit (Brevini, 2013, p. 111). The need to demonstrate 'distinctiveness' from the market, show 'added public value' compared to commercial offers and to provide 'predictability' for commercial competitors – the so-called triple test of public value – has been accompanied by what is known as the ex ante test, or the need to demonstrate all of these aspects of the new service in advance of its being launched (Brevini, 2013, pp. 114–15). These provisions are drawn from the Commission's competition policy and State Aid principles and have been applied as a response to complaints from commercial media organisations about publicly funded extensions of PSB encroaching upon their opportunities to develop profitable online and mobile services.

Debates about ex ante public value tests play out differently across the European Union, with stronger PSBs in countries such as Britain, Denmark and Germany being well placed to address such issues, whereas structurally weaker PSBs struggled to meet the bureaucratic hurdles that such tests created for the introduction of new online services. More generally, such a restrictive approach has been criticised for neglecting the important historical role that PSBs have played in providing a comprehensive media service, overstating their market failure rationales and constructing their standing in the media system as competitive threats to commercial media, rather than as facilitators of innovation and the formation of new markets (Karppinen, 2013, pp. 169–78; Berg et al., 2014).

We would argue that public value tests are more than simply a 'fad' (e.g. Lee et al., 2011), but constitute one attempt to develop a performance metric for PSMs that make use of public funds and have complex and sometimes conflicting organisational objectives. We can identify its roots in the neoclassical conception of market failure, and the stricture that investment in PSM is a form of government intervention in otherwise well-functioning commercial markets that can only be warranted where such market failures can be demonstrated through an ex ante public value test.

From the perspective of evolutionary/innovation economics, a major flaw with these tests is that they presume that the new media markets are relatively stable and that one can readily identify the private sector

initiatives that would be 'crowded out' by the entry of PSM development of new digital and online services. Cunningham (2013, p.
95) has argued that PSM has increasingly been engaged in 'a ... facilitative role of
performing experimental R&D for the system', while Martin and Lowe
(2014, p. 36) argue that by extending their offerings into online environments, PSMs are 'engaged in a logical, principled and appropriate
adaptation to a changing media marketplace, to the evidenced interests
of diverse publics'.

So while PSB may have been associated with genre innovation in
the context of universal access to its radio and TV services – think, for
instance, of the long-term impact of *Monty Python's Flying Circus*, which
the BBC first put to air in 1968, on television comedy – PSM is increasingly presenting its case for continued public subvention on the basis of
promoting digital innovation in 'a policy and innovation environment
in which the choice to innovate is no longer optional' (Cunningham,
2013, p. 108). With respect to innovation, evolutionary economics provides a different case for public service media than the more traditional –
and increasingly contested – market failure arguments of neoclassical
economics and the citizenship discourses of critical political economy.

The changing ecology of television

We have paid close attention to the non-market affordances of digital
media and communications in Chapter 4. But one of the major features
of change in this rapidly evolving landscape is the degree to which this
burgeoning form of media activity is being brought to market. This case
study tracks the major features of this dynamic change process which,
as one might expect, is primarily happening in the US 'hothouse', with
implications for TV systems around the world. We note how the different economic approaches we have canvassed in this book can contribute
to understanding the changes, while emphasising the applicability of
evolutionary economics approaches.

Analyses of the rate of change of the membership of the Fortune
500 (the largest United States companies) show clearly that the velocity
of turnover has increased as time has passed (Strangler and Arbesman,
2012). In contrast, there has been remarkable stability in business dominance in the screen industry. During the first half of the 20th century,
eight companies came to dominate film (Paramount, MGM, Fox, Warner
Brothers, RKO, Universal, Columbia and UA). Of these, only RKO fell
from grace, replaced within the oligopoly by Disney during the 1950s,

and MGM–UA slipped from the annual list of top 10 studio-distributors only during the 2000s. While shorter-lived, the oligopoly in broadcast television is even tighter, with CBS, NBC and ABC having dominated the TV landscape for almost 70 years. However, there is evidence that the established screen industries now face the most serious challenge in their history.

While Hollywood tried and failed to establish viable online distribution businesses from 1997 onwards, the new challengers (including Apple, Amazon, Google, Yahoo! and Netflix) are mostly very large companies outside the traditional media industries, drawing upon deep resources and employing IT-industry business models rather than Hollywood's premium-content and premium-pricing models. That these new challengers have been prepared to work around the content blocking tactics of the Majors by commissioning new content is to observe not only some deep Hollywood history repeating itself but also substantial change in the modes of presentation and distribution of content.

In the United States, Netflix and YouTube are estimated to account for about 50% of total Internet traffic. With YouTube now estimated to be worth up to US$21.3 billion (Cohen, 2013), and Netflix already referring to itself as the 'world's leading internet TV network', it is unsurprising that it is predicted that the annual value of North America's electronic home video market (pay-TV and over-the-top (OTT) streaming services) will surpass the cinema box office for the first time in 2017 (US$14.78 billion compared to US$13.50 billion). OTT services that deliver video over the Internet are growing rapidly, generating estimated revenues of US$17.4 billion in 2017, up from US$5.2 billion in 2012 (PwC, 2014). Internet advertising in the United States exceeded TV advertising revenues for the first time in 2013, amounting to US$42.8 billion, up 17% year on year, whereas TV advertising meanwhile turned over US$40.1 billion in 2013 (TBI Vision, 14 April 2014).

The annual revenues of the Majors (with their parent conglomerates) were 77.5% of those of the new players (Apple, Amazon, Google, Facebook, Yahoo!, Netflix) (US$249.69 billion vs. US$322.1 billion) in 2013. Figure 5.1 shows these relativities over the past decade.[1]

Where Google/YouTube, Apple's iTunes, Amazon and Yahoo! fundamentally differ from the incumbents is that they are Internet 'pure-play' companies that already had or have been able to develop a critical mass of online customers and thus possess extensive data on their past online search behaviour and purchasing habits. In addition, these companies have experience in marketing directly to their customer base, targeting

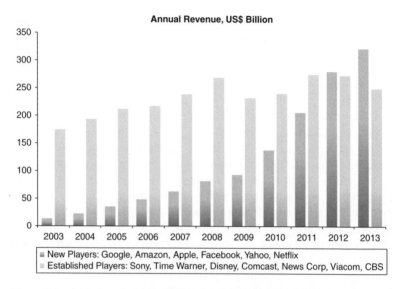

Figure 5.1 Annual revenue, established vs. new media firms, 2003–13
Source: Annual company filings with the United States Securities and Exchange Commission.

those most likely to be interested in a particular genre or programme based on web analytics of each individual's past behaviour and any product feedback that they may have provided. These differences optimise their chances of being able to formulate successful business models and better monetise screen content online.

This has produced a situation where, perhaps for the first time, the age-old truism of media economics, 'Nobody knows anything' (consumer preferences for media product are largely unknowable with any degree of accuracy), has been systematically addressed. Madrigal (2014) has documented the manner in which Netflix, one of the most successful new digital distributors, 'reverse engineered' Hollywood by meticulously analysing and tagging every movie and TV show in its immense catalogue, capturing hundreds of different movie attributes and stockpiling an unprecedented amount of metadata about Hollywood entertainment. And the data attached to 'Visually-striking Foreign Nostalgic Dramas' or 'Critically-acclaimed Emotional Japanese Sports Movies' is in turn combined with viewing habits of Netflix's more than 50 million subscriber base across nearly 50 countries. This data gives Netflix an advantage based on 'big data' in their efforts to produce their own content: 'Netflix has created a database of American cinematic predilections. The data can't tell them how to make a TV show, but it can tell them what they should be making. When they create a show like House of Cards, they aren't guessing at what people want' (Madrigal, 2014).

These leaders in IT, computing and social media are developing strategies – commissioning, channel branding, event programming, selling advertising to fit genres, audience demographics and even timeslots – just like TV networks. They are 'working around' content blocking tactics of the Majors by commissioning new content, facilitating substantial change in the modes of presentation and distribution, as well as types, of content. They are also leading in controlling the platforms that deliver content to larger and larger audiences across the second screens of computers and mobile devices.

YouTube has gone even further, commissioning content first within its Original Channel Initiative and then with multi-channel networks (MCNs) that have grown rapidly within the YouTube ecosystem. Among the largest are Fullscreen, Big Frame, Machinima, Maker, Defy Media, Stylehaul, CDS, BroadbandTV, Bent Pixels, Base 79, Revision3 and IGN. As content aggregators, MCNs seek to leverage scale advantages to attract advertisers while providing support, education and marketing services for the array of original content providers within their network. Just as the new platform providers are outsiders, our research conducted in early 2014 on the backgrounds of the founders and CEOs of major MCNs indicate that 14 out of the top 34 MCNs (in terms of size, scale and popularity on YouTube) had no movie, TV or music industry experience, so they were attitudinally unfettered by ingrained industry paradigms. The other 20 had top executives who had worked in content businesses, and several of these roles were for independents, not the major studios.

The scope and scale of change occurring in China bears direct comparison to the United States. China now claims the largest broadband user-base, the largest online population and the second-largest cinema market in the world – which is very soon to eclipse the United States. By mid-2014, China's Internet population stood at 641 million, a demographic dominated by youth and white-collar workers. With such a large Internet population, it is not surprising that much of the consumption of Chinese film and video occurs online. Yet while China's Internet population is large, only a small percentage is able to access Western video hosting services such as YouTube, Vimeo and Vine which are blocked by the government. Zhao and Keane (2013) also show that the introduction of the Administrative Provisions on Internet Audio-Visual Program Services in December 2007 resulted in a massive shake up of the audio visual market, killing off many of the illegal BitTorrent-based online video sites or forcing them to acquire a licence. Chinese net users are now encouraged to make use of approved online video sites; to date, the most prominent of these are 56.com, Ku6, LeTV, Youku (a merger of Youku and Tudou) and iQiYi (owned by China's largest search engine, Baidu).

Chinese Internet communities, particularly 'grassroots communities', willingly provided such sites with freshly generated content similar to the YouTube model. And because of the higher acquisition costs of foreign content, approved video hosting sites have been drawn towards Korean and Taiwanese content, which was cheaper and widely popular among viewers, as well as experimenting with alternative strategies such as in-house production. The most popular content genres in this regard are TV dramas, entertainment programmes and micro-movies featuring content that is culturally specific to East Asia and targeted at a youth demographic. Such content has led to more exposure opportunities for pan-Asian celebrities, and the use of this talent pool has become a vehicle to tap into the broader Asian pop culture community.

Community input into content creation as such represents a significant moment in the opening up of the Chinese mediasphere. The move towards producing original content is significant and demonstrates the attempts of the new content providers to differentiate themselves from the perceived 'national brand', that is, the widespread perception that Chinese audio visual content is generally unattractive, politically focused, genre-limited and skewing old. The fusion of East Asian culture together with programming innovations now flowing into China from international partners intent on securing a slice of the 'world's biggest audience' (Curtin, 2007) make this a mediasphere under construction. The competitiveness and volatility of the online content market forces the state to take reform of the media seriously. And for a nation eager to promote its soft power, the potential is immense, while at the same time raising unique challenges for the regime. In the past the state has contained its media by a combination of coercion and reward for performance. As the market gains confidence and finds its own way within the East Asian market, and as it draws investment and ideas from international partnership, the state will be pulled into this orbit of competition.

Media economics approaches

The question of the relevance of *neoclassical* approaches to the dynamics in this ecology has been raised in a rare example of the attempted application of such approaches from within media studies, Gregory Steirer's

(2014) study of UltraViolet. As we saw in Chapter 1, Steirer valuably emphasises that standard neoclassical analytical categories such as substitutable goods and switching costs can be applied to explain the strategies employed by the Majors as they attempted, through UltraViolet and the Digital Entertainment Content Ecosystem, to steer consumers away from Apple's iTunes and streaming towards their less proprietary system and electronic sell through (EST). However, the failure of UltraViolet to gain traction in the culture of the digital marketplace needs an historical, evolutionary perspective that emphasises the degree to which Hollywood incumbents have, at great cost and with extraordinary implications for ongoing corporate strategy, failed in the past and up to the present to successfully engage with digital culture and capture value from its challenges and affordances (Cunningham and Silver, 2013).

It is undeniable, in such a rapidly evolving, emergent market, that the co-evolving institutions that support, embed and correct its dynamic features are often lagging. An *institutionalist* approach might focus on the fact that contractual asymmetries, for example, abound and are the sites of regular struggle. The monetisation process laid out in these initiatives appears very attractive, but it is highly fraught, and is subject to similar issues that affect other new methods of creative and co-creative activity undertaken in proprietary spaces, such as massive multiplayer online games (MMOGs). These concern the status of intellectual property generation and the absence of natural justice and legal recourse when disputes arise. There is the plangent account of 'what it's like being sacked by a Google algorithm' (Winter, 2011) that tells the story of Dylan Winter, a freelance English journalist and filmmaker, and reveals rare details of the financial interactions between Google and the then 97th biggest reporter on YouTube globally and 7th in the United Kingdom. Despite being a very successful contributor to YouTube and valuable generator of attention to the ads placed next to his content by Adsense, Google's advertising placement company, Winter infringed a contract that was 'designed so that it was almost impossible not to break the Google rules' (Winter, 2011).

Vexed issues of contracting are actually the concerns of neoclassical, institutional *and* political economy approaches. The seriousness of the issue was visited on the industry during the Writers Guild of America Strike in 2007–8, when the WGA sought increased monetary compensation for the writers in comparison to the profits of the larger studios around three key areas: DVD residuals; jurisdiction in animation and reality TV and, perhaps most critically, new media. The latter concerned compensation for online delivery channels. At the resolution of the strike, the writers achieved success in that they were to receive a new percentage payment on the distributor's gross for digital distribution. It is now the case that, for example, Netflix's *House of Cards* is under the American Federation of Television and Radio Artists' jurisdiction, and Machinima.com's *Rapid Eye Movement* is under the Screen Actors Guild New Media agreement (Handel, 2012). The New Media Agreement in 2011 covers original and derivative entertainment productions made for initial release on new media platforms and also covers recognition and coverage, compensation, applicable provisions of the basic and television agreements, arbitration, reuse, initial release in traditional media, credit and reporting.

Critical political economy and *evolutionary proponents* would debate the significance of the changes underway. Political economy perspectives will tend to stress continuity (even as they also offer powerful accounts of the digital era in corporate capitalism, e.g. Fitzgerald, 2012; Fuchs, 2014), while evolutionary approaches will seek to assess the rates and qualitative dimensions of change. This feeds into how the media, communication and cultural studies discipline field hotly contests how to account for the rates and effects of digitally influenced change. Is it that we are 'both witnesses to and participants in the largest, most fundamental transformation in the history of the media since the advent of typeface, the moving image, and terrestrial broadcast transmission' (Levin, 2009, p. 258) or is the evidence for the supplanting of old by new 'sparse and thin' (Miller, 2010, p. 10) and ignores the way the new is folded into the old, adding to rather than killing it off? An evolutionary approach enables us to ask: how do we study the process and the rate of change? In this case of screen distribution, are there new players disrupting the established Hollywood oligopoly and, if so, with what effect? Is there evidence of disruption to business models? What has really changed if what we are seeing is the changing of the guard from one powerful oligopoly to another? What normative value do we accord to trends towards the formalisation and commercialisation of often previously amateur production and 'bottom-up' access for new content creators to wide distribution potential?

Screen scholarship has tended to focus on incumbency and on continuity rather than on the new players and change. According to Perren and Petruska (2012), most of the 'limited number of scholarly studies of Hollywood digital-distribution strategies thus far...have tended to focus predominantly on the continuities in business strategies and corporate practices across conglomerates' (2012, p. 106). It tends, however, to play down the 'widespread sense of chaos and confusion' (2012,

p. 106) within the citadels of media power. Perren's work (2010; and with Petruska, 2012) has focused on diametrically opposed corporate strategies (Disney and ABC's amity with Apple versus Time Warner's and HBO's enmity; and, even within the same company, News Corp's distributing *Glee* far and wide, but stamping down on any *ultra vires* circulation – or even independent discussion – of *Wolverine*). Holt (2013, p. 31) has pointed out that such conflict *within* conglomerates inhibit their capacity to respond effectively to the changes that surround them.

This is consistent with earlier observations from Dwayne Winseck, in Chapter 2, that political economy tends to underplay the uncertainty and risk – and failure rates – involved in most business activity under conditions of competitive market capitalism. In this case, there are powerful voices asserting the resilience of the Hollywood majors in the face of the digital challenge. Anita Elberse (2013) doubts that Chris Anderson's 'long tail' hypothesis can withstand the sort of scrutiny she applies to the resilience, indeed thriving dominance, of the blockbuster entertainment model invented by Hollywood and now being adopted in book publishing, music, opera and sport. Eli Noam (2010) argues that the 'industrial efficiency' of the Majors will see them not only survive but thrive. He bases this fundamentally on an exposition of the post-Fordist production arrangements that have evolved in Hollywood over recent decades, and the central belief that, in a field of burgeoning content and limited time for consumption, quality – Hollywood's blockbuster production values and budgets – will triumph. What Noam doesn't take account of is the bracing fact that Hollywood has almost no ownership stake in most of the new players and platforms, and the historical evidence that, at points of transition such as the early years of TV, audiences have been prepared to embrace quite different versions of quality when what is gained is convenience and innovation. Less programmatic is the work being conducted in the Media Industries Program and Connected Viewing Initiative at University of California Santa Barbara (Holt and Sanson, 2013), which manages to focus on the complex challenges faced by incumbents without pre-empting the question of their continued dominance.

But there is also significant variety, as well as competitive conflict, among the new players and it is incumbent on media analysts to differentiate carefully without assuming predictive powers. The threat to the incumbents posed by Google's video platform YouTube, the Amazon Prime Instant Video platforms in the United States and Europe, Netflix and Yahoo!Screen is real and present. Facebook and Apple (with iTunes, Apple TV and the much-rumoured iTV) have developed strategies that may see them also become content providers in Internet-delivered television. Intel and Microsoft have also invested heavily in establishing content distribution capacity as television migrates online. In terms of business strategy, there is also an important distinction between acquisition and commissioning models which focus almost exclusively on established professional content (Netflix, iTunes, Hulu and Amazon) and those which are facilitating low-budget but more creatively diverse, advertising-supported, professionalising content available from a wider range of sources either on YouTube or on other Internet video-hosting portals (Vimeo, Blip).

Despite this evidence for greater diversity, it is notable how rapidly the new content production environment has institutionalised along similar lines to the established TV production culture, which provides evidence for continuity and against radical change. Both individual content creators and the MCNs are in an interdependent battle with YouTube (a near-monopolist) over terms and conditions, revenue shares and the pros and cons of this newly minted TV ecology. Calacanis (2013) makes the advantages and disadvantages of 'working on YouTube's farm' clear. On the one hand, the sheer scale and quality of resource (free, global, HD video hosting with more than 1 billion users monthly, access to the largest advertising network in the world plus in-depth audience analytics and expert executives). On the other, high associated costs as YouTube takes its 45% cut of advertising revenues while providing no marketing. Content creators relying solely on YouTube – working essentially to burnish the YouTube brand – find it very hard to build a sustainable business.

Further evidence of well-established capitalist practice is seen in the beginnings of a shakeout among Multichannel Networks, and the purchase by Disney, reportedly for US$500 million in early 2014, of one of the leading MCNs, Maker Studios, that generates more than 5.5 billion views a month from a subscriber base of 380 million. Actions such as this suggest that the incumbents will seek to buy out major new media innovators, possibly also seeking to divorce them from their ties to threatening competitors like Google/YouTube.

We have looked at the interdependence of the informal and the formal in Chapter 4, as well as the formation of new markets based on that interdependence – social network markets. The rapidly evolving ecology of United States television that we profile in this case study is an outstanding example of social network markets. It has created very substantial new markets and new value, without necessarily destroying established markets. From a political economy perspective, however, this study of extremely rapid commercialisation from corporate origins platforming mostly amateur user-generated content might be asked: what value is being created, and what values reinforced, as YouTube first creates its Partners Program and then commissions content in its Original Channel Initiative, and now deals with Multichannel Networks in full-blown supply chains? One response might be to contrast the new television ecology with the recent history of other media sectors.

Federal Trade Commission Chairman Joe Leibowitz (2009) asks how journalism will survive the Internet age: is it undergoing 'creative' destruction or just destruction? His answer is the latter because, while the public's demand for the sort of information vital to democracy remains unabated, the business model on which news is delivered has broken down. Sellers of content that is a core public good can't be paid enough to remain in business, suggesting a fundamental market failure (see also McChesney and Pickard, 2011). However, the standard answer to market failure – for the government to step in – is problematic because this would compromise the independence of the 'fourth estate'. Another variant on creative destruction, *self*-destruction, is, according to Steve Knopper (2009), exemplified in the record industry's series of responses to the threat posed by digital file sharing.

We have focused in this section on online screen distribution as a case in the study of fast-moving, digitally influenced change. While we have found much to agree with Gray and Lotz's point that 'Television is neither "beating" nor "losing" to new media in some cosmic clash of technology; rather, television is an intrinsic part of "new" media' (Gray and Lotz, 2012, p. 3), we have suggested that there is more at stake than the 'continuity' scholars might lead us to believe. Television as we know it is neither dead nor dying. Television is being reinvented, but with significant differences and innovations.

With regard to ownership, control and business strategy, the new players we have canvassed represent potentially epochal change in what we have noted as, historically, remarkably stable oligopolies in film and television. Some of these new players massively outrank in size and scale the companies that have run film and television. Like all large-scale corporations, they are likely to use market power to seek to limit competition and many try to corral users inside walled gardens. While their revenue models, principally subscription VOD and advertising, are not new, the growing efficiency with which they are being implemented continues to grow steeply their revenue base, although the 'analogue dollars to digital cents' conundrum remains. Their business strategies, on the other hand, are definitely undercutting premium content and premium pricing Hollywood logics and the bulk bundling logics of cable. Through them, distribution of licit screen content has never before been so varied and accessible. They have provided platforms and implemented strategies that have seen a range of new types of professionalising content come to the fore. They are investing directly in content whereas hitherto it was mostly a case of aggregating others' content. Commissioned content providers come from a wide range of countries.

Conclusion

We have sought in this book to introduce a broader understanding of what economics might contribute to the media, communication and cultural studies discipline field. We have outlined the two dominant strands of media economics – the neoclassical mainstream and critical political economy – not to polemicise for one or against the other, but to suggest that the well-rounded media student should understand both, and also understand some limitations of each. We have provided a sustained attempt to apply institutional and evolutionary economics to the media, and their affiliated fields of information and innovation economics, in the context of observing that economics as a discipline is more diverse and heterogeneous than those outside the discipline commonly assume. At the same time, we recognise the challenges arising from the fact that, unlike neoclassical media economics or critical political economy, institutional and evolutionary economics have not had much of a focus on media.

Throughout the book, we have used case studies to indicate that these different economic paradigms are not just theories but also provide important practical insights into how media operate today. We have considered tablet PCs as an example of supply and demand in media markets; whether there has been a concentration of media ownership over time; the economics of digital platforms; how economic and other forms of power interact, with reference to the classic media mogul Rupert Murdoch, with a cultural superpower like Disney, and small versus big business; reasons for the contracting complexity in the media; broadcasting property rights; global media policy and governance; media piracy; and extended consideration of both PSM and the changing ecology of television.

We would suggest that the heterodox versions of economics we have canvassed here can assist media, communication and cultural studies with some of their current transdisciplinary dialogues and some of their recurring internal issues. We note that there are key thinkers who have contributed to these diverse economic traditions, including Thorstein Veblen, Max Weber and Joseph Schumpeter, and that links can be drawn between their insights from an earlier phase of capitalism to contemporary issues being addressed in new institutional economics, economic sociology and information and innovation economics. Moreover, these paradigms can address not only the traditional media industries and markets but challenges being presented by digital networks, convergent media and user-created media content.

At a deeper level, these heterodox versions of economics have attempted to reconnect their discipline to history and society. Leading exponents of heterodox economics, such as Richard Nelson and Sidney Winter, for example, claim that it 'has open frontiers, lives with other disciplines in what is recognizably the same intellectual world and has much to offer and to gain from trade' (2002, p. 42). We think that 'trade' with these brands of economics can help media, communication and cultural studies with, for example, its approach to a recurring issue such as technological determinism. Brian Arthur's (2009) account of the evolution of technology elegantly addresses the issue of technological determinism by insisting that physical technologies, social technologies and business strategy together shape how technologies evolve. How media fits into *long duree* historical change – to take the recurrent issue of the need to historicise the digital present – can be understood very much from the perspective of some of the major works in economic history, such as Schumpeter's *Business Cycles* (1939), which have come from heterodox economics. Manuel Castells' theory of the 'network society' (1996), highly influential in media, communication and cultural studies, has been explicitly derived from Schumpeterian 'long wave' theory.

We think that an appreciation of diverse strands of economics helps to better grasp contemporary challenges facing media industries and better understand media activity from a producer, consumer *and* critic's point of view. This may help the discipline move beyond what we consider to be is its 'blackbox' approach to firms, markets and economic value and values in contemporary capitalist economies. As an exciting transdisciplinary field of inquiry, media, communication and cultural studies has always sought to connect with subtending fields and thus extend its agendas, renew its relevance and maintain its balance between theoretical rigour and empirical reach. With some exceptions – most notably Winseck (2011) – it is notable that the field has not engaged in an extended debate about the types of economics appropriate to the contemporary media field. This has left the field largely with a fairly stale recycling of the neoclassical–critical political economy stand-off. Leading but diverse figures in the media, communication and cultural studies field, such as Larry Grossberg and Nicholas Garnham, have commented that this blind spot towards how economists are interpreting such changes in the media ecology has inhibited the discipline's advance.

Opening the 'blackbox' means having to deal with capitalism as a complex adaptive system, deeply conflictual in its processes and effects. Key figures in the history of heterodox economics, such as Veblen, Weber and Schumpeter – as well as the contemporary polymath Deidre McCloskey – have been clear that these conflictual dynamics have deep cultural roots and deep cultural effects. New York's New School for Social Research has established the Robert L. Heilbroner[2] Center for Capitalism Studies, and a Manifesto produced for its 'Capitalism Studies' states: 'We apprehend capitalism as both a system fundamentally grounded in violence *and* the most effective engine for bettering the material condition of mankind ever known' (Ott and Milberg, 2014). For media, we have seen that this means both accumulation (the new ecology of TV adds value for both producers and consumers) and annihilation (digital disruption is undercutting media practices which have important social and political functions such as journalism). We have seen that it can mean the further extension of the international division of labour into the sphere of media with the New International Division of Cultural Labor (NICL) as well as the judo moves taken by those countries, states and film agencies which have sought to produce a net benefit for their local industries from Global Hollywood.

We have noted (in Chapter 1) political scientist Robert Entman and economist Steven Wildman's rare attempt at 'reconciling economic and non-economic perspectives' between market and social value schools of thought, because 'the two are often so far apart in their assumptions and languages that they are unable to communicate with each other' (1992, p. 5). Entman and Wildman rehearse a range of trigger issues: for the market school, economic efficiency is a prime goal in itself and it is believed to bring social benefits, whereas the social value school emphasises that the social impact of media is such that it cannot, and must not be guided by economic efficiency alone. They recommend deeper engagement around normative ideas of diversity, on which both sides may begin to agree, and that governing metaphors like the 'marketplace of ideas' need renovation.

Whatever we might think of these recommendations more than 20 years on, that effort to bridge the gaping chasm across the disciplinary divide was heroic. We think that it remains timely that such a *rapprochement* occurs between media, communication and cultural studies, on the one hand, and economics, on the other. Attempts to bridge such deep theoretical and methodological divides are heroic at the best of times, and this short book will not settle all the arguments. But perhaps it will extend the frames of reference for those arguments beyond their current limits, which are inhibiting a better understanding of what is actually going on in contemporary media cultures, businesses, industries and markets.

Notes

Introduction

1. The 'marginal revolution' in economics refers to two developments that lay the groundwork for what we now term 'neoclassical economics'. First, there was a shift away from the concerns of classical economists such as David Ricardo with land, labour and capital as aggregate categories, towards interest in the decisions of individuals to produce, to consume, to work or to invest capital, which were derived from mathematical formulae. Second, there was a decisive shift away from seeing labour as the primary source and measure of value, towards seeing the value of commodities as an expression of the subjective preferences of individuals, with prices serving as a real-world proxy for such subjective judgements. As the identification of labour as the source and measure of value had come to be seen as providing the basis for a critique of the exploitation of labour by capital, particularly in the work of Karl Marx, the 'marginal revolution' also tended to be associated with implicit support for the existing socio-economic order, in contrast to the radical critique of the socialists. See Roncaglia (2005, pp. 278–96).
2. Space precludes an extended discussion of John Maynard Keynes's *General Theory of Employment, Interest and Money* (1936) and its enormous impact on the field of economics. In his biography of Keynes, Skidelsky (2003) identifies three insights from Keynes's work which have ongoing significance: (1) how pervasive uncertainty sets limits to rational behaviour on the part of market participants; (2) the importance of time in economics, and the barriers that existed to wages, prices and employment levels responding quickly to changes in macroeconomic variables such as effective demand or interest rates; and (3) the ongoing need for governments to manage key economic variables in order to both maintain high levels of employment and boost business confidence to invest.

1 Media Economics: The Mainstream Approach

1. The American Economics Association lists 18 fields into which scholarly work is classified. In addition, it has a 'Category Z' that consists of 'other special topics'. These include economics of the arts, economics of religion, economic

sociology and anthropology, and cultural economics. Media economics is not listed as a field at all, even though over 700 fields are listed. See AEA (2013).

4 Evolutionary Economics

1. The question of the generalisability of evolution has been the subject of debate since Herbert Spencer (1864) sought, in the immediate aftermath of *Origin of Species*, to extend evolution from biology to human culture and society. Contemporary studies include Hodgson and Knudsen (2010) on generalisability in general, with a stress on economics, Arthur (2009) on the evolution of technology, Boyd (2010) on the origin of stories and Burling (2007) on the origin of language.

5 Case Studies and Conclusion

1. Annual revenue filings do not allow for the disaggregation of content from diverse revenue sources; there is a mixture of revenue derived from media and non-media sources. For example, Apple's revenue includes that derived from hardware devices and iTunes receipts, while Amazon's includes revenue derived from all the goods and services it profits from. The disaggregation problem applies also to the Majors, with Sony's revenue including dividends from hardware manufacturing, and Disney's revenue extending beyond its vast media holdings to parks and resorts and many consumer products. Nevertheless, the comparison of a ten-year trend in overall revenue between the two camps maps modest growth for the incumbents against rapid and extraordinary growth for the new players.
2. Working at the New School, Robert Heilbroner (1999) wrote the last edition of one of the classics of economic history and thought, *The Worldly Philosophers: The Lives, Times And Ideas of the Great Economic Thinkers*.

References

Akerlof, G. (1970) The Market for 'Lemons': Quality, Uncertainty and the Market Mechanism. *Quarterly Journal of Economics* 84: 488–500.

Albarran, A. (2002) *Media Economics: Understanding Markets, Industries and Concepts* (Ames, IO: Iowa State University Press).

Albarran, A. (2010) *The Media Economy* (New York: Routledge).

Albarran, A., Chan-Olmsted, S. and Wirth, M. (eds.) (2006) *Handbook of Media Management and Economics* (Mahwah, NJ: Lawrence Erlbaum Associates).

Albarran, A. and Dimmick, J. (1996) Concentration and Economics of Multiformity in the Communication Industries. *Journal of Media Economics* 9(4): 41–50.

Alexander, A., Owers, J., Hollifield, A. and Greco, A. (eds.) (2004) *Media Economics: Theory and Practice* (Mahwah, NJ: Lawrence Erlbaum Associates).

American Economic Association (2013). JEL Classification System/EconLit Subject Descriptors. http://www.aeaweb.org/econlit/jelCodes.php?view=econlit, date accessed 3 February 2014.

Andrejevic, M. (2004) *Reality TV: The Work of Being Watched* (Lanham, MD: Rowman & Littlefield Publishers).

Andrejevic, M. (2007) *iSpy: Surveillance and Power in the Interactive Era* (Lawrence, KS: The University Press of Kansas).

Andrejevic, M. (2013) *Infoglut: How Too Much Information Is Changing the Way We Think and Know* (New York: Routledge).

Ang, I. (1985) *Watching Dallas: Soap Opera and the Melodramatic Imagination* (London: Metheun).

Armstrong, M. (2005) Public Service Broadcasting. *Fiscal Studies* 26(3): 281–99.

Arthur, B. (2009) *The Nature of Technology: What it is and How it Evolves* (London: Penguin).

Authors Guild v. Google Inc. Opinion 05 Civ. 8136 (Judge D. Chin) (2013) United States District Court Southern District of New York, 14 November. http://www.library.umass.edu/services/scholarly-communication/copyright/cases/google-books-case/, date accessed 12 April 2014.

Babe, R. E. (1995) *Communication and the Transformation of Economics* (Boulder, CO: Westview Press).

Bagdikian, B. (1983) *The Media Monopoly* (Boston: Beacon Press).

Bagdikian, B. (2004) *The New Media Monopoly* (Boston: Beacon Press).

Bakhshi, H. (2010) Beauty: Value Beyond Measure? Commission for Architecture and the Built Environment http://webarchive.nationalarchives.gov.uk/

20110118095356/http:/www.cabe.org.uk/files/people-places-hasan-bakhshi.
pdf, date accessed 21 April 2014.

Bakhshi, H., Freeman, A. and Hitchen, G. (2009) Measuring Intrinsic Value:
How to Stop Worrying and Love Economics. *Mission Money Models*, April.
http://www.britishcouncil.org/measuring_intrinsic_value-2.pdf, date accessed
21 April 2014.

Baldwin, R., Cave, M. and Lodge, M. (2012) *Understanding Regulation:
Theory, Strategy, and Practice* (2nd Edition) (Oxford: Oxford University
Press).

Ballon, P. (2014) Old and New Issues in Media Economics. In K. Donders,
C. Pauwels and J. Loisen (eds.), *The Palgrave Handbook of European Media Policy*
(Basingstoke: Palgrave), pp. 70–95.

Barnouw, E. and Gitlin, T. (eds.) (1998) *Conglomerates and the Media* (New York:
New Press).

Beinhocker, E. (2006) *The Origin of Wealth: Revolution, Complexity, and the Radical
Remaking of Economics* (London: Random House).

Belza, J., Foth, P., Purnell, J. and Zwillenberg, P. (Boston Consulting Group).
(2012) *Culture Boom: How Digital Media are Invigorating Australia*, March, commissioned by Google. http://www.bcg.com/documents/file101187.pdf, date
accessed 16 February 2015.

Benkler, Y. (2006) *The Wealth of Networks* (New Haven: Yale University Press).

Benkler, Y. (2011) The Unselfish Gene. *Harvard Business Review*. http://www.
clarityconsultants.com/wp-content/uploads/2012/07/2011_november_
unselfish_gene.pdf, date accessed 18 November 2012.

Benington, J. and Moore, M. (2011) Public Value in Complex and Changing
Times. In J. Benington and M. Moore (eds.), *Public Value Theory and Practice*
(Basingstoke: Palgrave), pp. 1–30.

Bennett, T. (1982) Theories of the Media, Theories of Society. In M. Gurevitch,
T. Bennett, J. Curran and J. Woollacott (eds.), *Culture, Society and the Media*
(London: Methuen), pp. 30–55.

Berg, C. E., Lowe, G. F. and Lund, A. B. (2014) A Market Failure Perspective on
Value Creation in PSM. In G. F. Lowe and F. Martin (eds.), *The Value of Public
Service Media* (Göteberg: NORDICOM), pp. 105–26.

Bettig, R. (1996) *Copyrighting Culture. The Political Economy of Intellectual Property*
(Boulder, CO.: Westview Press).

Bhagwati, J. (1993) *Protectionism* (Cambridge, MA: MIT Press).

Bharadwaj, K. (1990) Vulgar Economy. In J. Eatwell, M. Milgate and P. Newman
(eds.) *Marxian Economics* (London: Macmillan), pp. 373–76.

Boden, M. and Miles, I. (eds.) (2000) *Services and the Knowledge-Based Economy*
(London & New York: Continuum).

Bordwell, D., Staiger, J. and Thompson, K. (1985) *The Classical Hollywood Cinema:
Film Style and Mode of Production to 1960* (New York: Routledge).

Born, G. (2005) *Uncertain Vision: Birt, Dyke, and the Reinvention of the BBC*
(London: Vintage).

Boyd, B. (2010) *On the Origin of Stories: Evolution, Cognition, and Fiction* (Cambridge, MA: The Belknap Press).

Braithwaite, J. (2008) *Regulatory Capitalism* (Cheltenham: Edward Elgar).

Bresnahan, T. and Trajtenberg, M. (1995) General Purpose Technologies: 'Engines of Growth'? *Journal of Econometrics* 65(1, Special Issue): 83–108.

Brevini, B. (2013) *Public Service Broadcasting Online: A Comparative Study of PSB 2.0* (Basingstoke: Palgrave).

Bryman, A. (2001) The Disneyization of Society. *The Sociological Review* 47(1): 25–47.

Brynjolfsson, E., Hu, Y. and Smith, M. D. (2003) Consumer Surplus in the Digital Economy: Estimating the Value of Increase Product Variety at Online Booksellers. *Management Science* 49(11): 1580–96.

Brynjolfsson, E. and McAfee, A. (2011) *Race against the Machine: How the Digital Revolution is Accelerating Innovation, Driving Productivity, and Irreversibly Transforming Employment and the Economy* (Lexington, MA: Digital Frontier Press).

Burling, R. (2007) *The Talking Ape: How Language Evolved* (Oxford: Oxford University Press).

Calacanis, J. (2013) I ain't gonna work on YouTube's farm no more. *Launch.* 2 June. http://blog.launch.co/blog/i-aint-gonna-work-on-youtubes-farm-no-more.html, date accessed 2 June 2013.

Caldwell, J. T. (2008) *Production Culture: Industrial Reflexivity and Critical Practice in Film and Television* (Durham: Duke University Press).

Campbell, J. L. (1998) Institutional Analysis and the Role of Ideas in Political Economy. *Theory and Society* 27(4): 377–409.

Carey, J. W. (1989) *Communication as Culture: Essays on Media and Society* (New York: Routledge).

Castells, M. (1996) *The Rise of the Network* Society. Vol. I of *The Information Age: Economy, Society and Culture* (Malden, MA: Blackwell).

Catephores, G. (1994) The Imperious Austrian: Schumpeter as Bourgeois Marxist. *New Left Review* 205(1): 3–30.

Caves, R. (2000) *Creative Industries: Contracts Between Art and Commerce* (Cambridge, MA: Harvard University Press).

Chavance, B. (2009) *Institutional Economics* (London: Routledge).

Cheeseborough, H. (2006) *Open Innovation: Researching a New Paradigm* (Oxford: Oxford University Press).

Chenoweth, N. (2001) *Virtual Murdoch: Reality Wars on the Information Highway* (Melbourne: Vintage).

Choi, K. (2012) Disneyfication and Localisation: The Cultural Globalisation Process of Hong Kong Disneyland. *Urban Studies* 49(2): 383–97.

Christensen, J. G. (2011) Competing Theories of Regulatory Governance: Reconsidering Public Interest Theory of Regulation. In D. Levi-Faur (ed.), *Handbook of the Politics of Regulation* (Cheltenham: Edward Elgar), pp. 96–110.

Christensen, J. G. and Laegreid, P. (2011) The New Regulatory Orthodoxy: A Critical Assessment. In D. Levi-Faur (ed.), *Handbook of the Politics of Regulation* (Cheltenham: Edward Elgar), pp. 361–76.

Clegg, S., Kornberger, M. and Pitsis T. (2005) *Managing and Organizations* (London: Sage).

Coase, R. (1937) The Nature of the Firm. *Economica* 4: 386–405.

Coase, R. (1959) The Federal Communications Commission, *Journal of Law and Economics* 2: 1–40.

Coase, R. (1966) The Economics of Broadcasting and Government Policy. *American Economic Review* 56 (1/2): 440–7.

Coase, R. (1984) The New Institutional Economics. *Zeitschrift für die Gesamte Staatswissenschaft* 140: 229–31.

Cohen, J. (2013) YouTube Is Worth Up To $21.3 Billion. *Tubefilter.* July 2013. http://www.tubefilter.com/2013/07/29/youtube-valuation-worth-21-billion/, date accessed 17 August 2013.

Colander, D., Holt, R. and Rosser, B. (2004) The Changing Face of Mainstream Economics. *Review of Political Economy*, 16(4): 485–99.

Cole, K., Cameron, J. and Edwards, C. (1991) *Why Economists Disagree: The Political Economy of Economists* (London: Longman).

Collins, R. (2004) 'Ises' and 'Oughts': Public Service Broadcasting in Europe. In R. C. Allen & A. Hill (eds.), *The Television Studies Reader* (London: Routledge), pp. 33–51.

Compaine, B. (2001) The Myths of Encroaching Global Media Ownership. *Open Democracy.* 8 November. http://www.opendemocracy.net/media-globalmediaownership/article_87.jsp, date accessed 3 February 2014.

Compaine, B. (2005) *The Media Monopoly Myth: How New Competition is Expanding our Sources of Information and Entertainment* (New York: New Millennium Research Council).

Convert, B. and Heilbron, J. (2007) Where did the New Economic Sociology Come From? *Theory and Society* 36(1): 31–54.

Cowen, T. (2008) Why Everything has Changed: The Recent Revolution in Cultural Economics. *Journal of Cultural Economics* 32: 261–73.

Crowley, D. and Heyer, P. (1991) *Communication in History: Technology, Culture, Society* (New York: Longman).

Cunningham, S. (2012) Emergent Innovation through the Co-Evolution of Informal and Formal Media Economies. *Television and New Media* 13(5): 415–30.

Cunningham, S. (2013) *Hidden Innovation: Industry, Policy and the Creative Sector* (St Lucia: University of Queensland Press).

Cunningham, S. and Silver, J. (2013) *Screen Distribution and the New King Kongs of the Online World* (New York: Palgrave Macmillan).

Curran, J. (1990) The 'New Revisionism' in Mass Communication Research. *European Journal of Communication* 5(2): 135–64.

Curtin, M. (2007) Playing to the World's Biggest Audience: The Globalization of Chinese Film and TV (Los Angeles: University of California Press).

Dale, G. (2010) *Karl Polanyi: The Limits of the Market* (Cambridge: Polity Press).

Davies, G. (2004) *The BBC and Public Value* (London: Social Market Foundation).

Davis, H. and Scase, R. (2000) *Managing Creativity: The Dynamics of Work and Organisation* (Buckingham: Open University Press).

Dennett, D. (1995) *Darwin's Dangerous Idea: Evolution and the Meanings of Life* (London: Allen Lane).

Department of Culture, Media and Sport (DCMS) (2008) *Creative Britain: New Talents for the New Economy. Report prepared for Department for Business Enterprise and Regulatory Reform and Department for Innovation, Universities and Skills* (London: HMSO).

Dequech, D. (2003) Cognitive and Cultural Embeddedness: Combining Institutional Economics and Economic Sociology. *Journal of Economic Issues* 37(2): 461–70.

Dervin, B. (1993) Dallas Smythe: Epilogue as Prologue. In J. Wasko, V. Mosco and M. Pendakur (eds.), *Illuminating the Blindspots: Essays honoring Dallas W. Smythe* (Norwood, NJ: Ablex Publishing Corporation), pp. 401–09.

De Vany, A. (2004) *Hollywood Economics* (London: Routledge).

Dimmick, J. (2006) Media Competition and Levels of Analysis. In A. Albarran, S. Chan-Olmsted and M. Wirth (eds.), *Handbook of Media Management and Economics* (Mahwah, NJ: Lawrence Erlbaum Associates), pp. 345–62.

Douglas, M. (1986) *How Institutions Think* (New York: Syracuse University Press).

Dover, B. (2007) *Rupert's Adventures in China: How Murdoch Lost a Fortune and Found a Wife* (Edinburgh: Mainstream Publishing).

Doyle, G. (2006) Introduction. In G. Doyle (ed.), *The Economics of the Mass Media* (Cheltenham, UK: Edward Elgar), pp. xiii–xxvii.

Doyle, G. (2013) *Understanding Media Economics* (2nd Edition) (London: Sage).

Dredge, S. (2014) MIPTV Conference: Multichannel Networks Stake Claim to the Future of TV. *The Guardian*, Monday 14 April.

Dugger, W. (1990) The New Institutionalism: New But Not Institutionalist. *Journal of Economic Issues* 24(2): 423–31.

Dugger, W. and Sherman, H. J. (1994) Comparison of Marxism and Institutionalism. *Journal of Economic Issues* 28(1): 101–27.

Dunleavy, P. and O'Leary, B. (1987) *Theories of the State: The Politics of Liberal Democracy* (London: Macmillan).

Durkheim, E. (1964 [1910]) *The Division of Labour in Society* (New York: Free Press).

Earl, P. E. and Peng, T-C. (2012) Brands of Economics and the Trojan Horse of Pluralism. *Review of Political Economy* 24(3): 451–67.

Edquist, C. (1997) *Systems of Innovation: Technologies, Institutions and Organisations* (London: Pinter).

Ekelund, R. and Hébert, R. (2002) The Origins of Neoclassical Economics. *Journal of Economic Perspectives* 16(3): 197–215.

Elberse, A. (2013) *Blockbusters: Hit-making, Risk-taking, and the Big Business of Entertainment* (New York: Henry Holt and Co).

Elster, J. (2007) *Explaining Social Behavior: More Nuts and Bolts for the Social Sciences* (Cambridge: Cambridge University Press).

Entman, R. M. and Wildman, S. (1992) Reconciling Economic and Non- Economic Perspectives on Media Policy: Transcending the 'Marketplace of Ideas'. *Journal of Communication* 42(1): 5–19.

European Commission (2010) *Green Paper: Unlocking the potential of cultural and creative industries*, COM(2010) 183 (Brussles: EC).

Evans, P. (1995) *Embedded Autonomy: States and Industrial Transformation* (Princeton, NJ: Princeton University Press).

Evans, P., Rueschmeyer, D. and Skocpol, T. (1985) *Bringing the State Back In* (Cambridge: Cambridge University Press).

Ewan, S. (1976) *Captains of Consciousness: Advertising and the Social Roots of Consumer Culture* (New York: McGraw-Hill).

Fama, E. and Jensen, M. (1983) The Separation of Ownership and Control. *Journal of Law and Economics* 26: 301–25.

Fiske, J. (1989) *Understanding Popular Culture* (London: Unwin Hyman).

Fitzgerald, S. W. (2012) *Corporations and Cultural Industries: Time Warner, Bertelsmann, and News Corporation* (Plymouth: Lexington Books).

Flew, T. (2006) The Social Contract and Beyond in Broadcast Media Policy. *Television and New Media* 7(3): 282–305.

Flew, T. (2011a) Media as Creative Industries: Conglomeration and Globalization as Accumulation Strategies in an Age of Digital Media. In D. Winseck and D. Y. Jin (eds.), *The Political Economies of Media: The Transformation of the Global Media Industries* (London: Bloomsbury Publishing), pp. 84–100.

Flew, T. (2011b) Rethinking Public Service Media and Citizenship: Digital Strategies for News and Current Affairs at Australia's Special Broadcasting Service (SBS). *International Journal of Communication* 5: 215–32

Flew, T. (2012) *The Creative Industries, Culture and Policy* (London: Sage).

Foucault, M. (1991) Governmentality. In G. Burchell, C. Gordon and P. Miller (eds.), *The Foucault Effect: Studies in Governmentality* (London: Harvester Wheatsheaf), pp. 87–104.

Freedman, D. (2014) Metrics, Models and the Meaning of Media Ownership. *International Journal of Cultural Policy* 20(2): 170–85.

Freeman, C. (1987) *Technology Policy and Economic Performance: Lessons from Japan* (London: Pinter).

Freiberg, A. (2010) *The Tools of Regulation* (Sydney: Federation Press).

Fuchs, Christian. (2014) *Social Media: A Critical Introduction* (London: Sage).

Furubotn, E. G. and Richter, R. (2005) *Institutions and Economic Theory: The Contribution of the New Institutional Economics* (Ann Arbor, MI: University of Michigan Press).

Gabrys, J. (2013) *Digital Rubbish: A Natural History of Electronics* (Digital Culture Books: http://www.digitalculture.org/books/digital-rubbish/)

Galbraith, J. K. (1973) Power and the Useful Economist. *American Economic Review* 63(1): 1–11.

Garnham, N. (1979) Contribution to a Political Economy of Mass Communication. *Media, Culture & Society* 1(2): 122–46.

Garnham, N. (1987) Public Policy and the Cultural Industries. *Cultural Studies* 1(1): 23–37.

Garnham, N. (1990) *Capitalism and Communication* (London: Sage).

Garnham, N. (1995) Political Economy and Cultural Studies: Reconciliation or Divorce? *Critical Studies in Mass Communication* 12(1): 60–71.

Garnham, N. (2005) From Cultural to Creative Industries: An Analysis of the Implications of the 'Creative Industries' Approach to Arts and Media Policy Making in the United Kingdom. *International Journal of Cultural Policy* 11(1): 15–30.

Garnham, N. (2011) The Political Economy of Communication Revisited. In J. Wasko, G. Murdock and H. Sousa (eds.), *The Handbook of Political Economy of Communications* (Malden and Oxford: Wiley-Blackwell), pp. 41–61.

Garnham, N. and Fuchs, C. (2014) Revisiting the Political Economy of Communication. *Triple-C* 12(1): 102–141. http://www.triple-c.at/index.php/tripleC/article/view/553/534, date accessed 24 March 2014.

Gasher, M (2002) *Hollywood North: The Feature Film Industry in British Columbia* (Vancouver: University of British Columbia Press).

George, L. and Hogendorn, C. (2012) Aggregators, Search, and the Economics of New Media Institutions. *Information Economics and Policy* 24(1): 40–51.

Giddens, A. (1984) *The Constitution of Society: Outline of a Theory of Structuration* (Cambridge: Polity Press).

Giddens, A. and Held, D. (1983) Introduction. In A. Giddens and D. Held (eds.), *Classes, Power and Conflict: Classical and Contemporary Debates* (London: Macmillan), pp. 3–11.

Gilpin, R. (2002) A Realist Perspective on International Governance. In D. Held and A. McGrew (eds.), *Governing Globalization* (Cambridge: Polity Press), pp. 237–48.

Gintis, H., Bowles, S., Boyd, R. and Fehr, E. (2005) *Moral Sentiments and Material Interests* (Cambridge, MA: MIT Press).

Giroux, H. A and Pollock, G. (2010) *The Mouse that Roared: Disney and the End of Innocence* (Plymouth: Rowman & Littlefield Publishers).

Glasgow University Media Group (1976) *Bad News* (London: Routledge & Kegan Paul).

Golding, P. and Ferguson, M. (1997) *Cultural Studies in Question* (London: Sage).

Golding, P. and Murdock, G. (2005) Culture, Communications and Political Economy. In J. Curran and M. Gurevitch (eds.), *Mass Media and Society* (4th Edition) (London: Hodder Education), pp. 60–83.

Goldsmith, B., Ward, S. and O'Regan, T. (2010) *Local Hollywood: Global Film Production and the Gold Coast* (St Lucia: University of Queensland Press).

Gomery, D. (1989) Media Economics: Terms of Analysis. *Critical Studies in Mass Communication* 6(1): 43–60.

Goodwin, P. (1998) *Television Under the Tories: UK Broadcasting Policy 1979–1997* (London: Routledge).

Goodwin, P. (2014) The Price of Everything and the Value of Nothing? Economic Arguments and the Politics of Public Service Media. In G. F. Lowe and F. Martin (eds.), *The Value of Public Service Media* (Göteburg: NORDICOM), pp. 77–86.

Granovetter, M. (1985) Economic Action and Social Structure: The Problem of Embeddedness. *American Journal of Sociology* 91(3): 485–510.

Grant, P. (2011) The UNESCO Convention on Cultural Diversity: Cultural Policy and International Trade in Cultural Products. In R. Mansell and M. Raboy (eds.), *The Handbook of Global Media and Communication Policy* (Malden, MA: Wiley-Blackwell), pp. 336–52.

Gray, J. and Lotz, A. (2012) *Television Studies* (Cambridge: Polity Press).

Grossberg, L. (1995) Cultural Studies vs. Political Economy: Is Anyone Else Bored With This Debate? *Critical Studies in Mass Communication* 12(1): 72–81.

Grossberg, L. (2010) *Cultural Studies in the Future Tense* (Durham, NC: Duke University Press).

Grossman, E. (2007) *High Tech Trash: Digital Devices, Hidden Toxics, and Human Health* (Washington: Shearwater).

Hall, P. A. and Soskice, D. (eds.) (2001) *Varieties of Capitalism: The Institutional Foundations of Comparative Advantage* (New York: Oxford University Press).

Hall, P. A. and Taylor, R. (1996) Political Science and the Three New Institutionalisms. *Political Studies* 44: 936–57.

Hall, S. (1986) Cultural Studies: Two Paradigms. In R. Collins, J. Curran, N. Garnham, P. Scannell, P. Schlesinger and C. Sparks (eds.), *Media, Culture and Society: A Critical Reader* (London: Sage), pp. 33–48.

Hall, S. and Jacques, M. (eds.) (1989) *New Times: The Politics of Post-Fordism* (London: Lawrence & Wishart).

Handel, J. (2012) Pilots Overwhelmingly AFTRA for 4th Year in a Row. *The Hollywood Reporter*. 2 May. http://www.hollywoodreporter.com/live-feed/aftra-television-pilots-sag-287161, date accessed 14 April 2014.

Hardy, J. (2014) *Critical Political Economy of Media: An Introduction* (London: Routledge).

Hargreaves, I. (2011) *Digital Opportunity: A Review of Intellectual Property and Growth*. An independent report, May. http://www.ipo.gov.uk/ipreview-finalreport.pdf, date accessed 12 November 2012.

Hartley, J., Potts, J., Cunningham, S., Flew, T., Banks, J. and Keane, M. (2013) *Key Concepts in Creative Industries* (London: Sage).

Harvey, D. (2005) *A Brief History of Neoliberalism* (Oxford: Oxford University Press).

Havens, T., Lotz, A. and Tinic, S. (2009) Critical Media Industry Studies: A Research Approach. *Communication, Culture & Critique* 2(2): 234–53.

Hayek, F. A. (1945) The Use of Knowledge in Society. *American Economic Review* 4: 519–30.

Hayek, F. A. (1973) *Law, Legislation, and Liberty* (London: Routledge & Kegan Paul).

Hays, S. (1994) Structure and Agency and the Sticky Problem of Culture. *Sociological Theory* 12(1): 57–72.

Heilbroner, R. (1999) *The Worldly Philosophers* (7th Edition) (London: Penguin).

Herd, N. (2012) *Networking: Commercial Television in Australia* (Sydney: Currency Press).

Herman, E. and Chomsky, N. (1988) *Manufacturing Consent: The Political Economy of the Mass Media* (New York, NY: Pantheon).

Herman, E. and McChesney, R. (1997) *The Global Media* (New York: Panthenon).

Hesmondhalgh, D. (2013[2002]) *The Cultural Industries* (3rd Edition) (London: Sage).

Hickey, W. (2013) HBO: We Know You're Pirating 'Game Of Thrones' And That's Fine. *Business Insider Australia*, 9 August. http://www.businessinsider.com.au/time-warner-ceo-people-pirating-game-of-thrones-is-better-than-an-emmy-for-hbo-2013-8, date accessed 21 April 2014.

Higley, J. (2010) Elite Theory and Elites. In K. T. Leicht and C. J. Jenkings (eds.), *Handbook of Politics: State and Society in Global Perspective* (New York: Springer), pp. 161–76.

Hindess, B. (1989) *Political Choice and Social Structure: An Analysis of Actors, Interests and Rationality* (Cheltenham: Edward Elgar).

Hirschmann, A. O. (1970) *Exit, Voice, and Loyalty: Responses to Decline in Firms, Organizations, and States* (Cambridge, MA: Harvard University Press).

Hoa, T. V. J. and Ironmonger, D. (2005) Equivalence Scales: A Household Production Approach. In J. T. V. Hoa (ed.), *Advances in Household Economics, Consumer Behaviour and Economic Policy* (Hants: Ashgate Publishing), pp. 85–8.

Hobsbawm, E. J. (1979) *Industry and Empire* (Harmondsworth: Penguin).

Hodgson, G. (1993) Institutional Economics: Surveying the 'Old' and the 'New'. *Microeconomics* 44(1): 1–28.

Hodgson, G. (2003) The Hidden Persuaders: Institutions and Individuals in Economic Theory. *Cambridge Journal of Economics* 27(2): 157–75.

Hodgson, G. (2004) *The Evolution of Institutional Economics* (London: Routledge).

Hodgson, G. (2007) Meanings of Methodological Individualism. *Journal of Economic Methodology* 14(2): 211–26.

Hodgson, G. and Knudsen, T. (2010) *Darwin's Conjecture: The Search for General Principles of Social and Economic Evolution* (Chicago and London: University of Chicago Press).

Holt, J. (2013) Regulating Connected Viewing: Media Pipelines and Cloud Policy. In J. Holt and K. Sanson (eds.), *Connected Viewing: Selling, Streaming, & Sharing Media in the Digital Age* (New York: Routledge), pp. 19–39.

Holt, J. and Perren, A. (eds.) (2009) *Media Industries: History, Theory and Method* (Malden: Wiley-Blackwell).

Holt, J. and Sanson, K. (2013) *Connected Viewing: Selling, Streaming, & Sharing Media in the Digital Age* (New York: Routledge).

Horwitz, R. B. (1989) *The Irony of Regulatory Reform* (Oxford: Oxford University Press).

Hoskins, C., McFadyen, S. and Finn, A. (2004) *Media Economics: Applying Economics to New and Traditional Media* (Thousand Oaks, CA: Sage).

Ingham, G. (1996) Some Recent Changes in the Relationship between Economics and Sociology. *Cambridge Journal of Economics* 20(2): 243–75.

Innis, H. (1991 [1951]) *The Bias of Communication* (Toronto: University of Toronto Press).

Ironmonger, D. (2011) The Interaction Between Household and Market Work in Economic Downturns. *Dialogue* 30(1): 45–52.

Ironmonger, D. and Soupourmas, F. (2009) Estimating Household Production Outputs with Time Use Episode Data. *Electronic International Journal of Time Use Research* 6(2): 240–67.

Jacka, E. (2003) 'Democracy as Defeat': The Impotence of Arguments for Public Service Broadcasting. *Television and New Media* 4(2): 177–91.

Jackson, W. (2009) *Economics, Culture and Social Theory* (Cheltenham, UK: Edward Elgar).

Jenkins, H. (1992) *Textual Poachers: Television Fans & Participatory Culture. Studies in Culture and Communication* (New York: Routledge).

Jensen, M. and Meckling, W. H. (1976) The Theory of the Firm: Managerial Behavior, Agency Cost, and Ownership Structure. *Journal of Financial Economics* 3(4): 305–60.

Jin, D. Y. (2010) *Korea's Online Gaming Empire* (Cambridge, MA: The MIT Press).

Johns, A. (2010) *Piracy: The Intellectual Property Wars from Gutenberg to Gates* (Chicago: University of Chicago Press).

Johns, A. (2012) Adrian Johns on 'The Politics of Media Piracy'. Franke Forum, University of Chicago. http://www.youtube.com/watch?v=cdmBI7N5hIA, date accessed 25 April 2014.

Kapp, W. E., Berger, S. and Steppacher, R. (2012) *The Foundations of Institutional Economics* (London: Routledge).

Karabell, Z. (2014) (Mis)leading Indicators: Why Our Economic Numbers Distort Reality. *Foreign Affairs* 23(2, March/April): 90–101.

Karaganis, J. (ed.) (2011) *Media Piracy in Emerging Economies* (New York: Social Science Research Council).

Karppinen, K. (2013) *Rethinking Media Pluralism* (New York: Fordham University Press).

Katz, E. and Liebes, T. (1984) Once Upon a Time, in Dallas. *Intermedia* 12(3): 28–32.

Katz, E. and Liebes, T. (1990) Interacting with 'Dallas': Cross Cultural Readings of American TV. *Canadian Journal of Communication* 15(1): 45–66.

Keen, S. (2001) *Debunking Economics: The Naked Emperor of the Social Sciences* (London: Zed Books).

Kerstenetsky, C. L. (2000) Hayek: The Evolutionary and the Evolutionist. *Rationality and Society* 12(2): 163–84.

Keynes, J. M. (1936) *The General Theory of Employment, Interest and Money* (London: Macmillan).

Knee, J., Greenwald, B. and Seave, A. (2009) *The Curse of the Mogul: What's Wrong With the World's Leading Media Companies* (New York: Portfolio).

Knopper, S. (2009) *Appetite for Self-Destruction: The Spectacular Crash of the Record Industry in the Digital Age* (New York: Free Press).

Konings, M. (2013) Austerity's Redemptive Promise. In T. Bennett (ed.), *Challenging (the) Humanities* (Nth Melbourne: Australian Academy of the Humanities/Australian Scholarly Publishing), pp. 117–33.

Küng-Shankelman, L., Picard, R. and Towse, R. (eds.) (2008) *The Internet and the Mass Media* (Thousand Oaks, CA: Sage).

Lamberton, D. (2006) New Media and the Economics of Information. In L. A. Lievrouw and S. Livingstone (eds.), *The Handbook of New Media* (2nd Edition) (London: Sage), pp. 364–85.

Langlois, R. N. (1986) The New Institutional Economics: An Introductory Essay. In R. N. Langlois (ed.), *Economics as a Process: Essays in the New Institutional Economics* (Cambridge: Cambridge University Press), pp. 1–25.

Lash, S. and Urry, J. (1987) *The End of Organized Capitalism* (Madison: University of Wisconsin Press).

Lee, D., Oakley, K. and Naylor, R. (2011) 'The Public Gets What the Public Wants'? The Uses and Abuses of 'Public Value' in Contemporary British Cultural Policy. *International Journal of Cultural Policy* 17(3): 289–300.

Leibenstein, H. (1950) Bandwagon, Snob, and Veblen Effects in the Theory of Consumers' Demand. *Quarterly Journal of Economics* 64(2): 183–207.

Leibowitz, J. (2009) 'Creative Destruction' or Just 'Destruction' How Will Journalism Survive the Internet Age? Opening Remarks of Chairman Jon Leibowitz FTC News Media Workshop 1–2 December 2009. http://www.ftc.gov/sites/default/files/documents/public_events/how-will-journalism-survive-internet-age/091201newsmedia.pdf, date accessed 17 April 2014.

Levin, J. (2009) An Industry Perspective: Calibrating the Velocity of Change. In J. Holt and A. Perren (eds.), *Media Industries: History, Theory and Method* (Malden: Wiley-Blackwell), pp. 256–63.

Li, L. (2009) *Breaking Through: The Birth of China's Opening-Up Policy* (Oxford: Oxford University Press).

Lipsey, R. G., Carlaw, K. and Bekar, C. (2005) *Economic Transformations: General Purpose Technologies and Long Term Economic Growth* (Oxford: Oxford University Press).

Loasby, B. (1999) *Knowledge, Institutions, and Evolution in Economics* (London: Routledge).

Lobato, R. (2012) *Shadow Economies of Cinema: Mapping Informal Film Distribution* (London: BFI/Palgrave Macmillan).

Lobato, R. and Thomas, J. (2015) *The Informal Media Economy* (Oxford: Polity Press).

Loisen, J. (2012) Prospects and Pitfalls for Douglass North's New Institutional Economics Approach for Global Media Policy Research. In N. Just and M. Puppis (eds.), *Trends in Communication Policy Research: New Theories, methods and Subjects* (Bristol: Intellect), pp. 35–53.

Lundvall, B. -Å. (1988) Innovation as an Interactive Process: From User-Producer Interaction to the National System of Innovation. In G. Dosi, C. Freeman, R. Nelson, G. Silverberg and L. Soete (eds.), *Technical Change and Economic Theory* (London: Pinter), pp. 349–69.

Lunt, P and Livingstone, S. (2012) *Media Regulation: Governance and the Interests of Citizens and Consumers* (London: Sage).

Madden, G. G. and Cooper, R. (eds.) (2009) *The Economics of Digital Markets* (Cheltenham: Edward Elgar).

Madrigal, A. (2014) How Netflix Reverse Engineered Hollywood. *The Atlantic*. 2 January. http://www.theatlantic.com/technology/archive/2014/01/how-netflix-reverse-engineered-hollywood/282679/, date accessed 14 April 2014.

March, J. G. and Olsen, J. P. (1989) *Rediscovering Institutions: The Organizational Basis of Politics* (New York: Free Press).

Martin, F. and Lowe, G. F. (2014) The Value and Values of Public Service Media. In G. F. Lowe and F. Martin (eds.), *The Value of Public Service Media* (Göteburg: NORDICOM), pp. 19–40.

Maxwell, R. and Miller, T. (2012) *Greening the Media* (New York: Oxford University Press).

Mayer, V. (2011) *Below the Line: Producers and Production Studies in the New Television Economy* (Durham: Duke University Press).

McChesney, R. W. (1999) *Rich Media, Poor Democracy* (Urbana: University of Illinois Press).

McChesney, R. W. (2013) *Digital Disconnect: How Capitalism is Turning the Internet Against Democracy* (New York: Free Press).

McChesney, R. W. and Nichols, J. (2010) *The Death and Life of American Journalism: The Media Revolution that Will Begin the World Again* (Philadelphia: First Nation Books).

McChesney, R. W. and Pickard, V. (eds.) (2011) *Will the Last Reporter Please Turn out the Lights: The Collapse of Journalism and What Can Be Done to Fix It* (New York: The New Press).

McChesney, R. W. and Schiller, D. (2003) *The Political Economy of International Communication: Foundations for the Emerging Global Debate about Media Ownership and Regulation* (United Nations Research Institute for Social Development, Technology, Business, and Society Program).

McCloskey, D. (2006) *The Bourgeois Virtues: Ethics for an Age of Commerce* (Chicago: University of Chicago Press).

McCloskey, D. (2010) *Bourgeois Dignity: Why Economics Can't Explain the Modern World* (Chicago: University of Chicago Press).

McCloskey, D. N. (2013) Why Economics cannot Explain the Modern World. *Economic Record* 89, June: 8–22.

McCloskey, D. (Forthcoming) *The Treasured Bourgeoisie: How Markets and Innovation Became Ethical, 1600–1848, and Then Suspect*.

McCraw, T. K. (2007) *Prophet of Innovation: Joseph Schumpeter and Creative Destruction* (Cambridge, MA.: The Belknap Press of Harvard University Press).

McGuigan, J. (1992) *Cultural Populism* (London: Routledge).

McGuigan, J. (2009) *Cool Capitalism* (London: Pluto Press).

McKinsey (2011) Internet Matters: The Net's Sweeping Impact on Growth, Jobs, and Prosperity. *McKinsey Global Institute.* http://www.mckinsey.com/insights/high_tech_telecoms_internet/internet_matters, date accessed 24 March 2013.

McKnight, D. (2012) *Rupert Murdoch: An Investigation of Political Power* (Sydney: Allen & Unwin).

Meehan, E. and Wasko, J. (2013) In Defence of a Political Economy of the Media. *Javnost-The Public* 20(1): 39–53.

Melody, W. H. (1987) Information: An Emerging Dimension of Institutional Analysis. *Journal of Economic Issues* 21(3): 1313–39.

Melody, W. H. (2007) Cultivating Knowledge for Knowledge Societies at the Intersections of Economic and Cultural Analysis. *International Journal of Communication* 1: 70–8.

Merton, R. (1968) *Social Theory and Social Structure* (New York: Free Press).

Metcalfe, J. S. (1998) *Evolutionary Economics and Creative Destruction* (London: Routledge).

Metcalfe, J. S. and Miles, I. (2000) *Innovation Systems in the Service Economy: Measurement and Case Study Analysis* (Boston: Kluwer Academic).

Miller, T. (2008) Anyone for Games? Via the New International Division of Cultural Labour. In H. Anheier and Y. R. Isar (eds.), *The Cultural Economy, The Cultures and Globalization Series, vol. 2* (London: Sage), pp. 227–40.

Miller, T. (2010) *Television Studies: The Basics* (London: Routledge).

Miller, T., Govil, N., McMurria, J., Maxwell, R. and Wang, T. (2005) *Global Hollywood 2* (London: BFI).

Moody, J. B. and Nogrady, B. (2010) *The Sixth Wave: How to Succeed in a Resource-Limited World* (North Sydney: Vintage Books).

Mosco, V. (2005) *The Digital Sublime: Myth, Power and Cyberspace* (Cambridge, MA: The MIT Press).

Mosco, V. (2009) *The Political Economy of Communication* (2nd Edition) (London: Sage).

Munster, G. (1985) *Rupert Murdoch: A Paper Prince* (London: Viking).

Murdock, G. (1982) Large Corporations and the Control of the Communication Industry. In M. Gurevitch, T. Bennett, J. Curran and J. Woollacott (eds.), *Culture, Society and the Media* (London/New York: Methuen), pp. 114–47.

Murdock, G. (1990) Redrawing the Map of the Communication Industries. In M. Ferguson (ed.), *Public Communication: The New Imperatives* (Newbury Park: Sage), pp. 1–15.

Murdock, G. (2013) Communication in Commons. *International Journal of Communication* 7: 154–72.

Murdock, G. and Golding, P. (1973) For a Political Economy of Mass Communications. In R. Miliband and J. Saville (eds.), *Socialist Register* (London: Arnold), pp. 70–92.

Murray, S. (2005) Brand Loyalties: Rethinking Content Within Global Corporate Media. *Media, Culture and Society* 27(3): 415–35.

Nee, V. (2005) The New Institutionalisms in Economics and Sociology. In N. J. Smelser and R. Swedberg (eds.), *The Handbook of Economic Sociology* (Princeton, NJ: Princeton University Press), pp. 49–74.

Neil, A. (1996) *Full Disclosure* (Basingstoke: Macmillan).

Nelson, R. (1993) *National Innovation Systems: A Comparative Analysis* (Oxford: Oxford University Press).

Nelson, R. R. and Winter, S. G. (2002) Evolutionary Theorizing in Economics. *Journal of Economic Perspectives* 16(2): 23–46.

Noam, E. M. (2009) *Media Ownership and Concentration in America* (Oxford: Oxford University Press).

Noam, E. (2010) Hollywood 2.0: How Internet Distribution will Affect the Film Industry. In W. R. Neuman (ed.), *Media, Technology and Society* (Ann Arbor: University of Michigan Press), pp. 59–69.

North, D. C. (1990) *Institutions, Institutional Change and Economic Performance* (Cambridge: Cambridge University Press).

North, D. C. (1994) Economic Performance Through Time. *American Economic Review* 84(3): 359–68.

Osborne, D. and Gaebler, T. (1992) *Reinventing Government* (Reading, MA: Addison-Wesley).

Ostrom, E. (1990) *Governing the Commons: The Evolution of Institutions for Collective Action* (New York: Cambridge University Press).

Ostrom, E. (2005) *Understanding Institutional Diversity* (Princeton, NJ: Princeton University Press).

Ott, J. and Milberg, W. (2014) Capitalism Studies: A Manifesto, 17 April. http://www.publicseminar.org/2014/04/capitalism-studies-a-manifesto/#.U2BXxfmSxBk, date accessed 29 April 2014.

Ouellette, L. and Lewis, J. (2004) Moving Beyond the 'Vast Wasteland': Cultural Policy and Television in the United States. In R. C. Allen and A. Hill (eds.), *The Television Studies Reader* (London: Routledge), pp. 52–65.

Page, B. (2003) *The Murdoch Archipelago* (New York: Simon and Schuster).

Pang, L. (2006) *Cultural Control and Globalisation in Asia: Copyright, Piracy, and Cinema* (London: Routledge).

Pellow, D. and Park, L. (2002) *The Silicon Valley of Dreams: Environmental Injustice, Immigrant Workers, and the High-tech Global Economy* (New York: New York University Press).

Perren, A. (2010) Business as Unusual: Conglomerate-Sized Challenges for Film and Television in the Digital Arena. *Journal of Popular Film & Television* 38(2): 72–8.

Perren, A. and Petruska, K. (2012) Big Hollywood, Small Screens. In P. Snickars and P. Vonderau (eds.), *Moving Data: The iPhone and the Future of Media* (New York: Columbia University Press), pp. 103–23.

Pertierra, A.C. and Turner, G. (2013) *Locating Television: Zones of Consumption.* (London: Routledge).

Peters, B. G. (2012) *Institutional Theory in Political Science: The New Institutionalism* (New York: Continuum).

Picard, R. (1989) *Media Economics: Concepts and Issues* (Thousand Oaks, CA: Sage).

Picard, R. (2011a) *The Economics and Financing of Media Companies* (New York: Fordham University Press).

Picard, R. (2011b) Economic Approaches to Media Policy. In R. Mansell and M. Raboy (eds.), *The Handbook of Global Media and Communication Policy* (Malden, MA: Wiley-Blackwell), pp. 355–65.

Polanyi, K. (1957 [1944]) *The Great Transformation* (Boston: Beacon Press).

Posner, R. (2010) *The Crisis of Capitalist Democracy* (Cambridge, MA: Harvard University Press).

Potts, J. (2000) *The New Evolutionary Microeconomics: Complexity, Competence and Adaptive Behavior* (Cheltenham, UK: Edward Elgar).

Potts, J. (2011) *Creative Industries and Economic Evolution* (Cheltenham, UK: Edward Elgar).

Potts, J. and Cunningham, S. (2008) Four Models of the Creative Industries. *International Journal of Cultural Policy* 14(3): 233–47.

Potts, J., Cunningham, S., Hartley, J. and Ormerod, P. (2008) Social Network Markets: A New Definition of the Creative Industries. *Journal of Cultural Economics* 32(2): 167–85.

Powdermaker, H. (1950) *Hollywood, The Dream Factory: An Anthropologist Looks at the Movie-Makers* (London: Little, Brown).

Pung, C., Clarke, A., and Patten, L. (2004) Measuring the Economic Impact of the British Library. *New Review of Academic Librarianship* 10(1): 79–102.

PwC (2014) Filmed Entertainment, Global Entertainment and Media Outlook: 2013–2017, http://www.pwc.com/gx/en/global-entertainment-media-outlook/segment-insights/filmed-entertainment.jhtml, date accessed 17 December 2013.

Quiggin, J. (2010) *Zombie Economics: How Dead Ideas Still Walk Among Us* (Princeton, NJ: Princeton University Press).

Quiggin, J. (2013) The Economics of New Media. In J. Hartley, J. Burgess and A. Bruns (eds.), *A Companion to New Media Dynamics* (Malden, MA.: Wiley-Blackwell), pp. 90–103.

QUT CIRAC and Cutler and Company (2003) Research and Innovation Systems in the Production of Digital Content and Applications. Report for the National Office of the Information Economy. https://www.chass.org.au/papers/pdf/PAP20030901CG.pdf, date accessed 21 April 2014.

Reiss, J. (2013) *Philosophy of Economics* (London: Routledge).

Rao, A. (2013) The Economics of Media: Reviewing an Important Course. *This is Ashok: Reality in Bits: Economics, Technology, and Thought* (blog), 15 May. http://ashokarao.com/2013/05/page/3/, date accessed 17 April 2014.

Roncaglia, A. (2005) *The Wealth of Ideas: A History of Economic Thought* (Cambridge: Cambridge University Press).

Rosenberg, N. (2011) Was Schumpeter a Marxist? *Industrial and Corporate Change* 20(4): 1215–22.

Roy, W. G. (2004) Socializing Capital: The Rise of the Large Industrial Corporation in America. In F. Dobbin (ed.), *The New Economic Sociology: A Reader* (Princeton, NJ: Princeton University Press), pp. 433–56.

Ruggie, J. G. (1992) Multilateralism: The Anatomy of an Institution. *International Organization* 46(3): 561–98.

Rutherford, M. (1994) *Institutions in Economics: The Old and New Institutionalism* (Cambridge: Cambridge University Press).

Rutherford, M. (2001) Institutional Economics: Then and Now. *Journal of Economic Perspectives* 15(3): 173–94.

Samuelson, P. (1976) *Economics* (8th Edition) (New York: McGraw-Hill).

Sandqvist, U. (2012) The Development of the Swedish Game Industry: A True Success Story? In P. Zackariasson and T. L. Wilson (eds.), *The Video Game Industry: Formation, Present State, and Future* (New York: Routledge), pp. 134–53.

Schatz, T. (2010 [1989]) *The Genius of the System: Hollywood Filmmaking in the Studio Era* (2nd Edition) (London: Faber and Faber; Minneapolis: University of Minnesota Press).

Schiller, D. (1999) *Digital Capitalism: Networking the Global System* (Cambridge, MA: MIT Press).

Schiller, H. I. (1973) *The Mind Managers* (Boston: Beacon Press).

Schiller, H. I. (1976) *Communication and Cultural Domination* (New York: International Arts & Sciences Press).

Schiller, H. I. (1992 [1969]) *Mass Communication and the American Empire* (2nd Edition) (Boston: Beacon Press).

Schiller, H. I. (1996) *International Inequality: The Deepening Social Crisis in America* (London: Routledge).

Schlesinger, P. (1979) *Putting 'Reality' Together: BBC News* (London: Constable).

Schneider, F., Buehn, A. and Montenegro, C. E. (2010) New Estimates for the Shadow Economies all over the World. *International Economic Journal* 24(4): 443–61.

Schumpeter, J. (1934) *The Theory of Economic Development* (Boston: Harvard University Press).

Schumpeter, J. (1939) *Business Cycles: A Theoretical, Historical and Statistical Analysis of the Capitalist Process* (New York: McGraw-Hill Book Company).

Schumpeter, J. (1942) *Capitalism, Socialism, and Democracy* (New York: Harper Books).

Scott, A. J. (2008) Cultural Economy: Retrospect and Prospect. In H. Anheier and Y. R. Isar (eds.), *The Cultural Economy, Cultures and Globalization Series, Vol. 2* (Los Angeles: Sage), pp. 307–23.

Scott, J. (2013) *Social Network Analysis* (3rd Edition) (London: Sage).

Scott, W. R. (2014) *Institutions and Organizations: Ideas, Interests and Identities* (4th Edition) (Los Angeles: Sage).

Shah, A. (2009) Media Conglomerates, Mergers, Concentration of Ownership. *Global Issues*. Published 2 January. http://www.globalissues.org/article/159/media-conglomerates-mergers-concentration-of-ownership, date accessed 2 April 2014.

Shawcross, W. (2003) *Murdoch* (New York: Touchstone).

Shapiro, C. and Varian, H. (1999) *Information Rules: A Strategic Guide to the Network Economy* (Boston: Harvard Business School Press).

Simon, H. A. (1957) *Models of Man: Social and Rational; Mathematical Essays on Rational Human Behavior in Society Setting* (New York: John Wiley and Sons).

Sinclair, J. (2011) Branding and Culture. In J. Wasko, G. Murdock and H. Souza (eds.), *Handbook of the Political Economy of Communication* (Malden, MA: Wiley-Blackwell), pp. 206–25.

Siwek, S. E. (2006) *The True Cost of Motion Picture Piracy to the U.S. Economy*. Institute for Policy Innovation, Policy Report 186, September. http://www.ipi.org/ipi_issues/detail/the-true-cost-of-sound-recording-piracy-to-the-us-economy, date accessed 25 April 2014.

Skidelsky, R. (2003) *John Maynard Keynes 1883–1946: Economist, Philosopher, Statesman* (London: Penguin).

Skocpol, T. (1992) *The Political Origins of Social Policy in the Untied States* (Cambridge: Cambridge University Press).

Smelser, N. J. and Swedberg, R. (2005) Introducing Economic Sociology. In N. J. Smelser and R. Swedberg (eds.), *The Handbook of Economic Sociology* (Princeton, NJ: Princeton University Press), pp. 3–25.

Smith, A. (1991 [1776]) *The Wealth of Nations* (Amherst, NY: Prometheus Books).

Smith, T., Sonnenfeld, D. A. and Pellow, D. N. (2006) *Challenging the Chip: Labor Rights and Environmental Justice in the Global Electronics Industry* (Philadelphia: Temple University Press).

Smythe, D. W. (1960) On the Political Economy of Communication. *Journalism and Mass Communication Quarterly* 37(4): 563–72.

Smythe, D.W. (1977) Communications: Blindspot of Western Marxism. *Canadian Journal of Political and Society Theory* 1(3): 1–28.

Smythe, D. W. (1981) *Dependency Road: Communication, Capitalism, Consciousness and Canada* (Norwood: Ablex).

Sparks, C. (1986) The Media and the State. In J. Curran, J. Ecclestone, G. Oakley and A. Richardson (eds.), *Bending Reality: The State of the Media* (London: Pluto Press), pp. 76–86.

Spencer, H. (1864) *Principles of Biology* (London: Williams and Norgate).

Steirer, G. (2014) Clouded Visions: Ultra Violet and the Future of Digital Distribution. *Television and New Media*, published online 10 March: 1–14. DOI: 10.1177/1527476414524842. http://tvn.sagepub.com/content/early/2014/03/06/1527476414524842, date accessed 1 April 2014.

Stiglitz, J. E. (2010) *Freefall: America, Free Markets, and the Sinking of the World Economy* (New York: W. W. Norton & Co).

Stilwell, F. (2002) *Political Economy: The Contest of Economic Ideas* (Oxford: Oxford University Press).

Strangler, D. and Arbesman, S. (2012) What does Fortune 500 Turnover Mean? *Ewing Marion Kauffman Foundation,* http://www.kauffman.org/~/media/kauffman_org/research%20reports%20and%20covers/2012/06/fortune_500_turnover.pdf, date accessed 18 December 2013.

Streeter, T. (1996) *Selling the Air: A Critique of the Policy of Commercial Broadcasting in the United States* (Chicago: University of Chicago Press).

Stretton, H. (1987) *Political Essays* (Melbourne: Georgian House).

Stretton, H. (2000) *Economics: A New Introduction* (London: Pluto Press).

Sundaram, R. (2009) *Pirate Modernity: Delhi's Media Urbanism* (London: Routledge).

Swedberg, R. (2003) *Principles of Economic Sociology* (Princeton, NJ: Princeton University Press).

Sweney, M. (2012) Facebook 'Adds £2bn to UK Economy'. *The Guardian,* 24 January.

TBI Vision (2014) Web ad revenues surpass TV. *TBI Vision.* 14 April. http://tbivision.com/news/2014/04/web-ad-revenues-surpass-tv/261442/, date accessed 14 April 2014.

Thierer, A. and Eskelsen, G. (2008) *Media Metrics: The True State of the Modern Media Marketplace* (Washington: The Progress and Freedom Foundation).

Thompson, J. B. (1995) *The Media and Modernity* (Cambridge: Polity Press).

Throsby, D. (2001) *Economics and Culture* (Cambridge: Cambridge University Press).

Tinic, S. (2005) *On Location: Canada's Television Industry in a Global Market* (Toronto: University of Toronto Press).

Tracey, M. (1998) *The Decline and Fall of Public Service Broadcasting* (Oxford: Oxford University Press).

Turner, G. (2011) Surrendering the Space: Convergence Culture, Cultural Studies and the Curriculum. *Cultural Studies* 25(4–5): 685–99.

Turner, S. (2009) Shrinking Merton. *Philosophy of the Social Sciences* 39(3): 481–89.

Van Cuilenberg, J. and McQuail, D. (2003) Media Policy Paradigm Shifts: Towards a New Communications Policy Paradigm. *European Journal of Communication* 18(2): 181–207.

Veblen, T. (1961 [1909]) The Limitations of Marginal Utility. Reprinted in *The Place of Science in Modern Civilisation* (New York: Russell & Russell), pp. 231–51.

Von Hippel, E. (2006) *Democratising Innovation* (Cambridge, MA: MIT Press).

The Walt Disney Company (2012) *Fiscal Year 2011 Annual Financial Report and Shareholder Letter.* http://a.media.global.go.com/investorrelations/annual_reports/WDC-10kwrap-2011.pdf, date accessed 5 February 2014.

Wasko, J. (2001) *Understanding Disney: The Manufacture of Fantasy* (Cambridge: Polity).

Wasko, J. (2004) The Political Economy of Communications. In J. D. H. Downing, D. McQuail, P. Schlesinger and E. Wartella (eds.), *The Sage Handbook of Media Studies* (Thousand Oakes: Sage), pp. 309–29.

Wasko, J., Murdock, G. and Sousa, H. (2011) Introduction: The Political Economy of Communication: Core Concerns and Issues. In J. Wasko, G. Murdock and H. Sousa (eds.), *The Handbook of Political Economy of Communications* (Malden and Oxford: Wiley-Blackwell), pp. 1–10.

Watson, T. and Hickman, M. (2012) *Dial M for Murdoch: News Corporation and the Corruption of Britain* (London: Allen Lane).

Weber, M. (1978 [1922]) *Economy and Society* (2 vols.) (Berkeley, CA: University of California Press).

Wildman, S. (2006) Paradigms and Economic Frameworks in Modern Economics and Media Economics. In A. Albarran, S. Chan-Olmsted and M. Wirth (eds.), *Handbook of Media Management and Economics* (Mahwah, NJ: Lawrence Erlbaum Associates), pp. 67–90.

Williamson, O. E. (1975) *Markets and Hierarchies* (New York: Free Press).

Williamson, O. E. (1985) *The Economic Institutions of Capitalism* (New York: Free Press).

Williamson, O. E. (2000) The New Institutional Economics: Taking Stock, Looking Ahead. *Journal of Economic Literature* 38: 595–613.

Winseck, D. (2011) The Political Economies of Media and the Transformation of the Global Media Industries. In D. Winseck and D. Y. Jin (eds.), *The Political Economies of Media: The Transformation of the Global Media Industries* (London: Bloomsbury Publishing), pp. 3–48.

Winter, D. (2011) Adsense, No Sense at All – What it's Like Being Sacked by a Computer...*Duckworks 2011*. http://www.duckworksmagazine.com/11/columns/guest/winter/, date accessed 17 April 2014.

Wolff, M. (2008) *The Man Who Owns the News: Inside the Secret World of Rupert Murdoch* (New York: Broadway Books).

Zelizer, V. (1988) Beyond the Polemics on the Market: Establishing a Theoretical and Empirical Agenda. *Sociological Forum* 3(4): 614–34.

Zhao, J. and Keane, M. (2013) Between Formal and Informal: The Shakeout in China's Online Video Industry. *Media Culture & Society* 35(6): 724–41.

Zittrain, J. (2008) *The Future of the Internet (and How to Stop It)* (New Haven: Yale University Press).

Zucker, L. (1987) Institutional Theories of Organization. *Annual Review of Sociology* 13: 443–64.

Zweimuller, J. (2000) Schumpeterian Entrepreneurs Meet Engel's Law: The Impact of inequality on Innovation-Driven Growth. *Journal of Economic Growth* 5(2): 185–206.

Index

Note: The letter 'n' following locators refers to notes.